FALLING
OFF
THE
LADDER

HELEN HILL

A CIP catalogue record for this book is available from the British Library.

ISBN 978-1-9196385-0-8
eISBN 978-1-9196385-1-5

Edited by Erin Chamberlain
Cover design by Vanessa Mendozzi
Internal design by Hannah Beatrice
Proofread by Yasmin Yarwood

For my dad, my hero.
(And the only person to have fallen off an
actual ladder in front of me.)
Your endless support has pushed me on
when I thought I couldn't do it.
All my grit, determination and sarcasm I got from you.
Miss you so much.
Love, your Flybee Frances
X

And also, for my grandma.
One tough lady who has inspired us all.
I hope you and Grandad are dancing the night away.
X

LEAPERS PLAYLIST

As a musical theme unintentionally appeared throughout the book, so I have made a playlist based around the themes and stories that appear. And I have asked feature leapers from the website for their anthem of choice.

Prepare for a real mixture of uplifting choons, motivational rock roars and some total cheese.

Scan this Spotify code in the app or search for Falling Off The Ladder to listen.

NOTE

Throughout the book I often refer to 'the corporate world'. I am using this as a catch-all term (alongside 'employment' and the 'career ladder'), to mean any type of employment when working for others – be it a large or small organisation, education, public or private sector. It keeps things simple and sometimes feels clearer than 'employment'. After all, even when working for ourselves, we are in employment too. Just the better kind.

CONTENTS

INTRODUCTION

WHAT IS THIS BOOK ABOUT?

Falling Off The Ladder is a self-help book of sorts. It's the guide I wish I had had when I furiously launched myself into full-time self-employment.

I had no clue as to what I was going to do and no idea where my head was. I needed advice, and I needed it quick. I had to swiftly pick myself up, dust myself off, wrap my head around what had happened, and go out and profess to be an 'expert', even though at the time I felt like nothing but a failure.

This is not a 'how to' guide to the practicalities of setting up a business – there are plenty of books like that already out there (take a look at the ones I recommend in the resources section at the back of the book). This book is about getting your head out of the mentality of working for others and living by their rules. It is about learning how to be the ruler of your own empire and thrive.

It is a book about starting out in a new business and doing it on your own terms. To work out what those terms even are. It is about picking up your confidence and starting again. It is rediscovering the 'real you' and unleashing it so you can build a business that reflects an accurate version of you, and you finally feel comfortable in your work. It is about letting your personality and skills shine – no more pretending to be someone else. It is about building your reputation and getting a steady stream of work and clients who appreciate you for you. The aim of this groundwork being to increase your chances of winning work through being yourself and communicating (and believing!) the value you can offer.

This book is about learning how to be the ruler of your own empire and thrive

The career ladder is not for everyone and there are alternatives out there for those who feel it is not a good place for them to be. I was one of those people, and I couldn't see a way out for so long. Even though I worked for myself part time for about 10 years I never thought it was something I could do full time. However, discovering self-employment transformed me from a hysterical hyperventilating hyena hiding in the toilets, as the latest panic attack took hold, to a semi-confident happy bunny who even sometimes thinks 'I'm bloody good, me.'

Ultimately, I want fellow self-employed peeps to know they are not alone, that there is a whole fabulous network out there who have felt the same – and who are ready to help one another along. I want to help others experience the transformation I have experienced. I want to help others to realise that there is a working world out there where you don't have to feel beaten down, patronised, lost, unhappy, stuck and all the myriad of other ways in which I have heard the corporate world and employment explained. There is a world of freedom, flexibility and contentment out there waiting for those who take the leap from the ladder.

WHO IS THIS BOOK FOR?

This book is for you if you feel lost in your career and are debating the leap into self-employment, or you have recently made it. Or maybe you have been working for yourself for some time, but still carry around the toxic demons from prior employment and would like to excise them pronto.

It is for you if you feel like you can't be yourself when working for others, or if you've realised the career ladder is not for you. It's for you if you are fed up of trying to fit in and pretending you are something you are not.

It is okay to be you and do it your way

It is for you if you have had a squiggly career because you have never quite felt that you belong and you feel like you are constantly coming up against blocks to any form of progression up the ladder.

It is for you if you don't feel like you fit the one-size-fits-all mould into which we are supposed to squish (ahem, distort) ourselves. Maybe it has resulted in you feeling like a total failure at times. You feel undervalued, unappreciated, frustrated, and know there must be a better way.

You just want to use your skills in the way you want, to be creative, to work to your values, and have a work life that is flexible for your needs. You want to define your own terms, rediscover your passion, and get balance back in your life.

You may have a lot of recovering to do to re-establish your confidence and you want to finally find a place where you can be yourself without judgement and reprimand.

It is for anyone that needs to hear that it is okay to be you and do it your way. If you would like to feel the strength of a community in helping you get back to being yourself. If you want to escape the forced fun that is company away days and endless meetings.

It is for you if you would like the guidance of a broken-in freelancer who has been there, done that and tested the waters for you to get some tips in turning things around.

It is for anyone having a wobble. Who's had a wobble. Who feels a wobble coming.

Are you nodding furiously?

Then let's begin.

AUTHOR PLEA

I am not a therapist or mental health professional. The content of this book has been gained from my multitude of experiences and what has worked for me, testing out the advice of many others. I've employed and experimented with aspects from the fields of mindfulness, therapy and cognitive behaviour therapy (CBT). I've explored the teachings of self-help gurus and well-being practitioners – my learnings have been wide and varied.

If you struggle with depression, anxiety or panic attacks, or any other severe warning signs and mental health issues, please do ensure you have a support system in place and know where you can find help.

Have an emergency plan, and discuss it with a trusted friend, partner or family member.

Talk.

Get help.

Ring someone.

Anyone.

Please do not struggle alone.

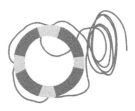

IT'S NOT JUST MY STORY

As I wrote this book, I asked some of my fellow self-employed and freelancer peeps to give me their input – and all answered with a resounding yes.

I had hoped to include all their stories in full, but it turns out the stories of my colleagues and friends is a book's worth in itself, so extracts appear throughout the book and you can access their full stories on the website.

To access this bonus content, go to fallingofftheladder.com/stars and enter the password FOTLstars21.

SCAN ME

Their stories are all worth your time – they are full of so much combined wisdom to both learn and take comfort from.

If you would like to connect with any of these fabulous people and learn more about their businesses, you can find their details below. Do go and say hi.

- Francesca Baker – copywriter and marketer
  And So She Thinks
  www.andsoshethinks.co.uk
- Giles Metcalfe – freelance self-employed digital marketer
  Giles Metcalfe Digital Marketing
  www.gilesmetcalfedigital.co.uk

- Pavitra Baxi – freelance translator
  www.pavitrabaxi.com
- Jo Watson – freelance copywriter, editor and trainer hired by people who want personality in their project. Also a speaker, someday author, and minor LinkedIn celebrity. agoodwriteup
  www.agoodwriteup.com
- Joelle Byrne – business strategist, passive income generation, multi-revenue streams, automation
  www.joellebyrne.com
- Sophie Cross – freelance marketer and writer at Thoughtfully and Freelancer Magazine
  www.thoughtfully.co.uk
  www.freelancermagazine.co.uk
- Craig Wright – technical writer
  Straygoat Writing Services Ltd
  www.straygoat.co.uk
- Matt Drzymała – copywriter and owner of Indelible Think Copywriting
  www.indeliblethink.co.uk
- Kate – this contributor's name has been changed at their request to remain anonymous. (Just be glad I gave you a sensible name, 'Kate'.)

MY STORY: FALLING FACE FIRST, JUST FOR A CHANGE

I fell off that bloody ladder. Hard.

Not even arse first. But flat on my face.

I was humiliated, exhausted and felt like a failure.

I had no idea what I was going to do next. BUT, I can honestly say, it was the best thing to ever happen to me.

It took until I was 35, and a lot of job changes, to finally find my fit.

The world of employment is a chaos of contradictions, guessing games and changing yourself to fit a mould

The world of employment is a chaos of contradictions, guessing games and changing yourself to fit a mould. And despite being a good worker and having a lot to offer I never seemed to get it right. I just had to watch as less-experienced colleagues got promotions handed to them on a plate. They were mouldable. Willing to work in a certain way, to do what they were told. They never questioned anything or rocked the boat. They were happy to be micromanaged.

I had spent a lifetime trying to do all the right things, putting in 1,000 per cent and for what? It got me nowhere. Throughout my roles in the design industry and education I have consistently been told to be less me and my efforts seemed to be a bad thing. My emotions certainly were.

- Worried about the student suffering domestic abuse, or the one who's just lost a parent in tragic circumstances?
  You worry too much; you just have to keep a distance.

- Having panic attacks in the toilets?
  You're too emotional and just can't handle it, and this is so unprofessional. Have you tried to take a Calms tablet? They helped my aunt's brother-in-law's cousin. How about you have a meditation break at 2pm on a Tuesday?
- Standing up for yourself when accused of dropping the ball with a project you knew nothing about?
  Well, aren't you defensive/aggressive/unprofessional?
- Struggling with a health condition?
  There doesn't look anything wrong with you. Are you sure you have it?

All these comments (or, should I say, accusations?) have been said to me at some point.

Additionally, I have been on the receiving end of continual contradictions where I just never found a balance that pleased others. I'd be told off for talking too much in the open-plan office one moment, then dragged into a room to be told I was pulling the mood down the next. This was all while the delightful combination of health issues, insomnia, stress and long commutes left me feeling exhausted (or defeated) and struggling to stay awake.

I was told to be honest about how I was feeling when it came to my health. Then my candour would be used against me, and I would be told I was being too honest and should keep my feelings to myself.

I was told to stop working so hard and doing overtime as I was exhausted and stressed, but then more tasks were assigned to my role (with no additional pay, obviously) or deadlines were reduced.

One minute I was told I was too passionate (I'm still not seeing how that is a bad thing), then the next minute my passion and dedication were used to their advantage.

The corporate world and its infamous ladder claim to offer so much – security, progression, opportunity, teamwork – but my reality was different. My personality didn't fit. My emotions didn't fit.

Ultimately, I was not a robot.

And humans were not welcome.

The odd one out

I was the classic overachiever at school and university (if we ignore a minor blip at A levels – I totally took the wrong subjects for me. Je suis not good at le français). As an adult, however, I wandered aimlessly from job to job, always feeling the expectation that companies wanted me to be someone else – to be a robot, a sheep, to never question anything or have ideas of my own. My personality was too daft, not serious (boring) enough, and eventually I lost that side of myself.

I had always felt at odds with the workplace, but I couldn't ever put my finger on how or why. I certainly knew something was wrong and that I was uncomfortable. I knew that I didn't quite fit the mould – but didn't understand why. I'd go on company away days and see everyone else throwing themselves into cringe-inducing activities involving acting, singing and the dreaded role play, and I would shrink into the shadows hoping to be unnoticed. Or if

The corporate world and its infamous ladder claim to offer so much – security, progression, opportunity, teamwork – but my reality was different

alcohol was available, get drunk just to deal with the situation, and that's never the best plan. I seemed like the odd one for actually preferring the idea of sitting at my desk working.

Right from the beginning of my career things didn't seem right.

Fresh out of university in my first job as a designer, my boss (also the owner of the business) pointed at me and declared to a co-worker, "She's not attractive. Her tits aren't big enough." The same boss repeatedly tried to set up traps to get us (only the girls) to fail them so he could tell us off. He made constant sexist comments, and a lot of racist ones. Yet, the colleague who would drop his trousers in front of the floor to ceiling window to shock people walking by was applauded for his efforts. When you are struggling with confidence, in your first 'proper job' and outnumbered by very blokey blokes, it is hard to stand up to these things, even if you know it's not right.

Fast forward 15 years and I felt no further on, no nearer to finding a place where I fitted in. I had bounced from business to business with renewed enthusiasm. I got my hopes up each time, only to realise that nothing ever changed. You can change the office but you can't change the culture of work. It had gotten to the point where I felt truly lost, alone and confused. I knew that I knew my stuff, that I was a bloody hard worker, but what was it all for? I was hitting roadblocks at every turn.

I lost hope.

I no longer saw the point in giving my all, but I couldn't stop. It isn't in me to do half a job, or to not care. I couldn't just switch off the ambition, determination or passion.

I started to feel completely defeated, constantly plagued by thoughts that I 'should' be somewhere further in my career. I

13

'should' be higher up the ladder. I 'should' know what I want to do. But I didn't and I wasn't. The more stressed I got, the harder it was to see a way through.

Eventually it built to what is probably classed as a breakdown. It was certainly a meltdown of epic proportions.

You can change the office but you can't change the culture of work

I ended up off sick repeatedly over a period of six months and during the last of the absences I received a letter from my employer – a letter that I maintain to this day should never have been sent – and it was clear I couldn't even recover at home in peace without conflict. I was already living in fear of the mail thanks to a series of written confirmations of every conversation coming through the letterbox.

Though receiving that last letter was the final tipping point and destroyed me that day, I am now grateful for it. It prompted me to immediately send an email to hand in my notice. Enough was enough. I was no longer willing to let people tear me apart. Something had to change. I had no idea what I was going to do, but I knew my first step was to say, "No more".

After already having had so many false starts, I knew I had to start again. And I had to do it while putting myself back together.

To this day I can still recall the sense of relief, euphoria, freedom that came from pressing send.

A weight was finally lifted.

Launched into the abyss

The day I handed my notice in was also the day I was contacted by a recruiter via LinkedIn about a contract job. I had never really heard of this (except in relation to gangsters putting a contract hit out on someone) and so hadn't considered this way of working as an option. After some back and forth my interest was piqued. I went for the job, figuring it would be a great gap filler while I figured out what I was going to do long term. And within a couple of days I had an interview and secured the contract on the spot.

Hallelujah!

It was agreed with my employer that I didn't have to work my notice and I spent a few weeks resting, pulling myself together and researching the world of sole trader versus limited companies and umbrella companies. I switched UnlikelyGenius™ from a little side business where I tinkered about with the occasional logo to being a full-time business. I fully expected this would just be a temporary measure and that I would have to be looking for a new permanent role alongside the contract.

But that didn't happen.

That first contract role was intimidating, terrifying even. I was constantly told I was the 'expert', when I felt far from even achieving amateur status. I was working with a team of well-established contractors who knew their stuff. I was also in an all-male environment – a team of great guys who were very confident and assured in what they were doing – the very opposite of what I felt. And there was many a power struggle between them. I was working in ways I hadn't experienced before – with Agile processes, scrum masters, and the like. It was a world full of jargon and acronyms, which no one explained to me as I was an 'expert'.

But I asked questions, learnt from them and fed off the team's confidence. That role gave me time to recuperate. As it was also an onsite contract, it had the added benefit of being a good stepping stone from permanent employment to self-employment in an office with a structured workday, to then finally having flexible self-employment working from home.

However, it wasn't all plain sailing. There were some difficulties in that contract role especially in relation to one person who seemed to sense my fragility and prey on it. Who was just too in your face and probing, about both professional and personal matters. She managed to constantly hit a nerve and I started to withdraw and go back into that inner hiding place, putting the defensive walls up. Looking back, I am

I was constantly told I was the 'expert', when I felt far from even achieving amateur status

not sure it was intentional. It was partly just her personality, and she clearly didn't understand the work our team was doing, or the role of a content designer, and she started to cause problems for us. I would avoid being around her and try to get out of meetings with her. I was not strong enough yet to deal with her.

The relationship totally broke down and my only option was to move on.

Turning it around

I left that role just as we went on a big trip to Norway, where I spent a lot of time pondering my next move.

Before we left, I had started to make sure my visibility was increased again, and to refine my online profiles. While scrolling through LinkedIn one day I saw a post from a recruiter asking if anyone was available for an eLearning project. I raised my hand and the next day had a phone interview from our Airbnb in Bergen, to the backdrop of an Elton John concert at the castle nearby and with Graham loitering in the background with a beer, supposedly trying not to listen. Not off-putting at all!

Again, I won the job on the spot.

I returned off holiday, started the job the next day and have never stopped since. The steady stream of contracts continued to come my way, with many clients also repeatedly coming back for more. Working from home was giving me the flexibility and headspace I needed to rebuild myself and find a way of working that was right for me. Now I cannot see ever working another way.

Self-employment is the place where I have finally found my tribe and where I feel understood, where I finally fitted in. Where I have finally managed to be happy and back to feeling myself.

Admittedly, that place is mostly also an online world – but it is one full of freelancers, business owners and similarly minded people. These people feel more real to me than many of the friends I have ever had. They are dedicated, determined, ambitious people. And they are so bloody lovely. They have had similar experiences and problems, and many of them feature later in this book. We all have a story of our own and have huge empathy for one another. We openly share skills and ideas, provide a brain to bounce ideas off, and cheerleading services or a well-time GIF for a bad day. We have virtual brews, sarcastic banter and occasionally, if lucky (and pandemics aside), get to meet up for a drink of something stronger.

I don't call myself an 'expert' or an 'entrepreneur' (or any of the gazillion other 'preneurs). I will never utter the word influencer <shudder> or claim to be out there hustling. (I still don't even know what those last two mean other than generally being famous for nothing.) I don't 'crush it' in the gym at 5am and I'm certainly not working from any exotic locations. But I am working hard, being brave, being open to new opportunities and pushing myself – maybe too hard at times.

In reality I am a big child who loves trips to the zoo, am an obsessive mumbun to two ridiculously fluffy rabbits (hence their feature on the cover) and can regularly be found partying the only way I know how – curled up under a blanket in my pjs with Prosecco and a book or one of my crochet/weaving/other crafty projects.

I do a top-quality range of dinosaur impressions (poses, not sound effects), I bloody love a sloth and I can injure myself on the most ridiculous things, even those meant to be soft and fluffy.

Seriously.

I cut my thumb open changing the duvet cover last week.

(Are you realising the book title's double meaning now?)

My long-suffering other half's regular exclamations of "You're such a child" and "What have you done now?" can be heard daily, while he rolls his eyes so far back in his head I fear they may never return.

It turns out this approach to life is not serious enough for corporate land or working for others. It does not a lifeless robot make. But on entering the world of self-employment, all this can be embraced. In fact, it is often applauded.

I get feedback that I have made processes enjoyable and fun while nailing the work. Strangers and remote contacts message to tell me that I am an inspiration. People earlier on in their journey get in touch and ask for advice as I am approachable and (unfortunately not paraphrasing here) "though totally daft, you know your stuff". I'll take that, thank you.

The feedback I receive now from my clients speaks volumes about the change that I have undertaken since escaping the clutches of permanent employment. The testimonials citing me to have all the things I was repeatedly told I was lacking – patience, leadership, resilience, flexibility – or that were seen as weaknesses – being caring, passionate, creative.

Three years later and I am now averaging two and a half to three times the highest wage I ever took in a full-time permanent role and I have a bank of repeat customers. I am invited to guest blog, run webinars and workshops, speak at events, be on live interviews and be a guest on podcasts. I have won awards and have a great presence or following on social media. And more importantly for the business, I am now pretty solidly booked for up to a year in advance for project work and have taken on a bank of sub-contractors to help out when needed.

Self-employment is the place where I have finally found my tribe, and where I finally fitted in

I never envisaged myself in this place, and still must pinch myself to believe it.

I just wanted an easier life where I could be me. Where I was not made to feel ashamed or like a failure every day. Where I could account for my health needs – we'll get onto that – and didn't have to feel guilty for going to almost weekly medical appointments. As an aside, it is no coincidence that since working for myself my health has improved dramatically, the appointments are every six to twelve months now and I have only had three days off sick in three years. In fact, I've had no sick days since working from home permanently, where I am safely away from everyone's germs.

Though, at time of writing, I have only been in full-time self-employment for just over three years, there has been such a stratospheric change in me, my confidence and my happiness that I wanted to explore how this has come about in the hope that it may help others.

This book is my journey. It has its ups and downs. It contains my story but also the story of others I have met in the wonderful world of freelancing. We each have a different tale to tell.

There have been happy tears, sad tears, tears of laughter, frustrated tears, tired and delusional tears, and indescribable tears of not having a clue why they are even happening. Beautiful connections made and trolls fought off (luckily the former outweighing the latter). Contracts won, clients lost. Friends made and connections lost.

Come join the tribe, and let's smash those ladders to smithereens

You may not agree with all of it. Hell, you might not agree with any of it. But this book details what has worked for me, and I deeply hope that by sharing my experiences, some of it will work for you too.

I certainly haven't done everything right along the way, but I have learnt some truths. My hope now is to continue that journey with you.

Come join the tribe, and let's smash those ladders to smithereens.

This is an interactive journey.

The book is filled with activities and prompts to get you thinking and taking action, and I hope there will be parts of the stories included that inspire you and get your grey matter buzzing.

So, grab a notebook and pen or your favourite notes app, and let's get started.

PART 1

SOMEONE GREASED THE RUNGS!

The career ladder promises us all so much. Stability. Structure. Opportunities for advancement. It can also present a myriad of problems, as the promises turn out to be a con. The real kicker is that it usually tries to convince you that the problem is **you**.

You are made to feel that you are intolerant, impatient, lack resilience, don't fit in, don't have the right skills or enough drive to succeed. The nature of an employed work life, for me at least, has been to endure and weather a whole barrage of criticisms that have imprinted onto my brain. It is designed to make us doubt ourselves and remain at the lowest rungs of the ladder, with defeat and frustration snapping at our heels.

Even those who don't have a hugely negative experience with toxic workplaces, bullying and the like can feel despondent, suffocated, anxious and unmotivated. They can find themselves stuck in a life of uninspiring back-to-back meetings. Meetings about having a meeting. Meetings about the meeting you just had.

There is little room for creativity and it requires a certain level of arse-kissing

It can be a rigid, lifeless world where everything is fixed and there is little room for creativity and development. It also requires a certain level of arse-kissing – which I just wasn't willing to take part in. I have integrity, ideas, opinions, a work ethic. But they were not appreciated. Being me rocked the boat. It was 'questioning authority'. On more than one occasion I would be bounding with excitement at an idea – only to be grounded with a resounding no!

I once suggested a different way of approaching a project, which I felt could be something great, especially for the learners who would be taking the course. My approach would help us to experiment with software in new ways. It was a way of making the end result much more innovative and exciting ... but I was shot down.

"There's no money in the schedule for that."

"That would take longer than the allocated time."

"It's all too ... uncertain. Untested."

"Just do what you've been asked."

In other words, it was different to how we ALWAYS did things.

A few days later in a meeting a manager piped up suggesting the very idea I had put forward. As if it was their own idea. No credit given. No mention of the fact that I had pretty much word for word made this proposal. And the final kicker – the project was given to someone else to do. I knew I couldn't stand up for myself and say anything. I would receive more backlash. So, I left the resentment stewing. Festering. Building momentum, adding to the pile that was already there.

It's that crushing kind of situation – on repeat – which increased my stress levels, my despondency and left me feeling at a loss.

And I'm not the only one. I've gathered the stories of some other self-employed peeps and they related similar experiences.

Francesca describes her time in employment as "the relentless workload. Never-ending pressure. Bullying tactics. Not much fun. It just exacerbated my feelings of not being good enough".

Matthew's story speaks of being powerless when working for others, where toxic work cultures and bullying left him feeling like he had no voice.

Giles tells me how he never felt like he fitted in. "I always felt like a square peg being forced into a round hole and getting hammered down when I still couldn't make it work. I struggled with overload and having to adapt to a working environment and hours that I blatantly wasn't suited to. I was often in trouble for 'underperforming' or the first to be let go when redundancies were in the offing."

And Kate's experiences speak volumes too. "I started to get frustrated with doing tasks for the sake of it, with agendas set by others with no input, and any attempts at questioning being deemed unhelpful or defensive." She felt under constant scrutiny – always feeling that she was being held up against the ideals and opinions of those above her. People that never fully accepted her way of thinking – it didn't match theirs, so it was deemed wrong.

We have all tried to ascend to the supposed lofty heights of the career ladder many times in different roles and industries, yet there are remarkably common themes to all our stories.

The reason I have had such a squiggly career is due to my determination to progress – to achieve success the way society defines it. I kept looking for a new route, thinking I was just in the wrong industry, or wrong organisation. I would surely find my place if I just kept going. I would find the place where I – and my skills – fitted in and was valued.

But it never happened. I ended up becoming increasingly fraught, depressed and anxious.

I went from graphic designer, to lecturer, to teaching assistant, to learning centre manager, to content designer, to instructional designer, to a different definition of content designer, all while running UnlikelyGenius™ as a side hobby to earn a bit of extra cash. Then came the winner – the self-employed learning and content designer extraordinaire.

In just the first two years as a full-time freelancer, I had had more success (by my definition not by society's), earned more money and become so much happier than I ever got close to achieving in 13 years working for others.

So, how did I get there?

You can still grieve all the hopes you had for your career

The first step was to change my mindset. To acknowledge where I was and move on from all my previous experiences – good and bad – and make sure I was not carrying my emotional and physical baggage forward into the business. I started to realise there was a process to work through.

In all my varied and baffling employments, I have observed seven phases in the process of falling (or leaping) off that wobbly, wonky career ladder. These phases echo the well-known stages of grief – denial, anger, bargaining, depression and acceptance. I think this is because walking out of a career can raise similar emotions to grief. Even if you want to go. Even if you see no alternative. Even if you're happy to go, or maybe even expected it.

You can still grieve all the hopes you had for your career in that world, all the future(s) you had planned out in your mind. You can miss your colleagues, or the opportunities you believe you have lost. You can feel disappointment at the wasted time and energy, and forlorn at the idea of starting again.

Not everyone's journey will follow all the phases and you may find different phases more challenging than I did. You may miss some entirely or make a conscious decision to quickly leap over some. But by being aware of the steps, you can identify the causes of your emotions, see how far you have come, see what lies ahead, and you can help remove a few bumps in the road.

So, before we start to look at how to rocket you off in your solo career, let's explore where you are coming from and where you currently stand, by working through the following stages:

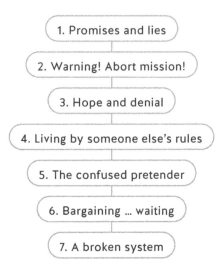

1. Promises and lies

2. Warning! Abort mission!

3. Hope and denial

4. Living by someone else's rules

5. The confused pretender

6. Bargaining ... waiting

7. A broken system

STAGE ONE: PROMISES AND LIES

> "You've made it. Welcome to the glam world of advertising and marketing. Drinks all the time. Expenses tabs. Enjoy the party."
> *Francesca*

It's an often-seen side of business life. We see it in films and television shows, read about it in books, sometimes even get glimpses of it ourselves. It's what we all aspire towards, right? And this is how Francesca describes her initial welcome into the world of advertising and marketing ... before the reality hit home.

The career ladder promises us all so much.

It promises the security of permanent roles, paid holidays and structured hours. It promises that we will be part of a team, that we will work together for something brilliant. Businesses pride themselves on their mission statements and harp on about their inclusive cultures. They describe their successes as a group effort, where everyone gets credit and plays their part. It promises that there will be opportunities for progression, and healthy regular wages to go with it. It promises a pension with employer contributions. Sometimes you even get a health plan.

Then there are the free lunches and brews. Beers after work. Colleagues and office banter. Chats over a brewing kettle or the water fountain. Corporate away days and team building. For many, even an office romance.

But what if all this turns out to be a smokescreen?

What if health plans were implemented to try and counteract the culture of a business that is driving their employees to sickness?

What if their claims of sharing credit are only where it benefits them (hello, awards submissions) and otherwise glossed over?

What if there is progression, but only for those who are deemed the chosen ones?

What if there is a toxic culture of bitching over that water fountain? Loudly. So others can hear.

What if all those things that used to be deemed benefits, such as pensions, are dwindling anyway and not worth a tenth of what they used to be?

What if the idea of 'forced fun' (team building activities) fills you with a rage that only the Hulk has previously achieved?

What if?

What if?

What if?

My experience of corporate promises is that they were empty – they just didn't deliver. Not just that, this way of working chewed me up until I was no longer recognisable and didn't actually know who I was any more.

So, why do we do it?

Well, from a young age we are taught this is what we do. We go to school and college, we are increasingly pushed towards university, and then we get employed by others. We are told that if we work hard, life will be plain sailing. We will love what we do and we will magically progress. We are led to believe you need experience first before contemplating working for yourself – if that is ever an option. It is often only later in our working lives that we start to realise there are other options out there.

This belief of how work was meant to be was so ingrained in me that I tried and tried. With every fall I picked myself back up and tried again, believing that the right opportunity for me was out there somewhere.

Even though I was freelancing on the side, it was just tinkering with low-paid jobs. I didn't even contemplate that I could have a full-time business.

We are told that if we work hard, life will be plain sailing. We will love what we do and we will magically progress

Every time I tried a new avenue to get to the magical, mystical land of opportunity I fell further into the pit of despair, feeling like a failure. I felt like I had wasted a lot of time and money on three(!) degrees. (Not to be confused with singing trio The Three Degrees ... that would have been a hell of a career change!)

I got angry at myself for repeatedly getting my hopes up.

Angry at others for not giving me a chance.

Angry at the world for keep sending me in a direction that didn't work for me.

Employers are looking for that specific type of person. Someone to fit their mould. To adapt themselves to an established culture, with no flexibility required on their part. It's all on you.

Looking back, I can see that with each new direction I took I had started to get increasingly anxious, but also more determined. That just meant the let-downs were even more crushing each time. I fell from a higher rung with a bigger bump every time. It was a hard cycle to break.

I was careering into my mid-thirties and had still not found my way. I felt so far beyond the time of life where we believe we should have our shit together. And obviously social media was telling me that everyone else indeed did have their shit together, with precision and skill.

For all its promises, I realise now that we give up a lot to be on that career ladder: independence, creativity, thoughts, expression, freedom, happiness, control. That's a delicious cake mix I am not willing to give up.

We give up a lot to be on that career ladder: independence, creativity, thoughts, expression, freedom, happiness, control

Instead, I found a ginormous helping of guilt, shame, disappointment, bullying, aggression, sexism and discrimination, with a massive side dish of anxiety and a buffet of depression.

These are not small things to trade. It adds up. And certainly not a worthy trade-off for the promises of a job.

I'd see the system working for others and start to think, well I MUST be the problem then. I must be a waste of space and destined to just stay at the bottom level. And, of course, no business is going to turn round and reassure you, "Nooo, it's us. We must do better."

My confidence was destroyed and the accusatory way in which things were thrown back at me made me hide how I was really feeling. I stopped being open. I attempted (very unsuccessfully) to mask the acute pain I was in. I played things down, maybe a bit too successfully as I was then accused of lying about the existence of my health condition(s). I pushed myself through presenteeism – turning up for work even when I knew I should have taken it off sick. I just couldn't cope with another back to work interview and conversation about my absences or another letter in the mail.

I would think, "I do a good job, I work hard, I use my skills well. I have given everything. More than everything. I have given my soul and my sanity. Why is it not good enough for me but it is for others?"

The situation became an uncontrollable cyclical beast.

The more stressed I felt and the more I was guilted about time out for medical appointments, the sicker I became. I tried to spread out appointments more despite needing them frequently, or I tried to avoid them altogether. My fatigue increased to the point that I was struggling to stay awake at my desk, or while driving. I had to switch to commuting by train whenever I could, but that took twice as long and so ended up just as exhausting (and well, Northern Rail ... I say no more). My resilience dropped. It didn't take much to become frustrated and panicky. I doubted everything about myself, and when endless negative, snarky comments were then levelled at me, I cemented them as truth in my brain. I believed what they said.

When I worked in education, sometimes I just wasn't even allowed to go to hospital appointments and was told I had to rearrange them for in the holidays, even though I had already waited months, or even years, to get the appointments. When your employer values a minor inconvenience of an hour out of the office over your health, you know you have a problem.

The cycle whipped me up and spat me out. I was having almost daily panic attacks and was in a severe amount of pain every minute of the waking and sleeping day, accompanied by a never-ending cycle of chronic exhaustion and insomnia. There was an increase in daily symptoms of a long-term health condition. I was at serious risk of damaging my physical and mental health (even more) in the long term.

The 'promises' were no longer good enough.

SOMEONE GREASED THE RUNGS!

Though 'the letter' I mentioned in the introduction to this book was the point that tipped me over the edge, there was no single defining moment that led to leaving that world. It was a build-up of all these events and more over a long period of time. A series of disappointments, in myself and others. I realised no one had my back (apart from those busy sticking a knife in it). I had been too trusting, too honest – and it was used against me. I was not playing the game correctly. I don't think I was even in the game.

This treatment of health conditions is a familiar one to many freelancers and forms a shocking part of Matthew's story. "I was signed off with stress. I suffered from depression and my epilepsy wasn't controlled at the time. When I was hospitalised after suffering a seizure in work, I was made fun of and ridiculed all the time. I reached a point where I just wanted to walk in front of a train, I was so low."

Though (hopefully) not many of us have experienced this level of brutality and preying on the vulnerable, it is more common than we realise. The undercurrent of exclusion, bullying and holding back those with health conditions is a major contributor to many people walking out of employment. Indeed the Culture Economy report[1] states that "21 percent of British people left a job due to toxic workplace culture in 2020". That is an incredible number of people uncomfortable at work.

Looking back, I now realise that all those things the career ladder promises are a smokescreen, and despite all fears to the contrary I have actually found everything it promised in self-employment, as have many others.

In self-employment I have found opportunities and progression, just in a different form to that in permanent employment. Instead of climbing the rungs of a greasy ladder I can dictate my own definition of success (we'll come to this

later) and development. I can make my own adventures. I can take many things on at once and see where I end up. I have the freedom to experiment, grow and learn.

If 2020 and the COVID pandemic has taught us anything, it is that no job is 'secure'. The world can flip on its axis in totally unpredictable ways, industries can collapse and suddenly all the promises count for nothing.

Looking back, I now realise that all those things the career ladder promises are a smokescreen

Sure, freelancing can be overwhelming at times, and some find it lonely. But those challenges are yours to overcome, and there are lots of solutions out there to help you. The challenges are yours to decide the best way through. And the successes are yours too. There is so much satisfaction in that alone.

I am learning to make promises to myself. It sounds a bit 'fluffy', but when I make sure I am happy, motivated and engaged in my work, I do my best work. My clients benefit from that. I promise myself lots of self-development, and time engaging with other freelancers and creatives. I promise myself rewards and treats. I have made a new promise to myself that this year I will only take on work that brings me joy or intrigues me – no longer saying yes just because of the dosh.

When we are in charge, we can make whatever promises we like to ourselves and set our own goals. And if we break them – well, reward yourself anyway. For the intention. The attempt. When you stick to them, you can have an even bigger prize.

You're the boss now. No one can say no.

What promises and lies have kept you in employment?

What have you sacrificed to be in employment – now or in the past?

Could you get this back in self-employment? How would you make sure you do?

STAGE TWO:
WARNING! ABORT MISSION!

If you have found yourself in the toxic underbelly of employed life, there are a few little signs you may start to notice. Signs that all is not well. That you are not coping. That it is having a detrimental effect on your health. Others might even start to point them out for you and say things like "you're not happy". But you can still be in denial that things are not that bad and will change for the better. That it is just a blip, things will definitely change.

When this stress becomes constant, your mind and body will start to tell you.

You defence mechanisms will be on high alert.

You may get paranoid (though you may actually be justified in these thoughts).

You may feel like there is no more point in trying.

Or like there is no way out, no hope, no escape.

You could have lost all pleasure in what you used to love doing and not feel yourself any more.

Maybe you're unusually emotional, or the opposite – feeling numb. Maybe even veering between the two.

You are probably exhausted and feel like others have all the power, but you have no energy to fight back.

You are compromising who you are for others.

It all just feels ... wrong.

When you realise the discord between your values and a company's values are so cavernous, there is little you can do to pull that back. Other than press eject. Get the hell out.

They aren't going to change, so it is up to you to. But if you already feel like you have tried everything, what more is there to do? Where can you go from here?

Are you willing and able to drop your values, principles, beliefs, ethics, morals, style, processes, opinions or whatever else don't align?

Change your mind, your being, your presence to fit in?

Lose the very essence of you?

Taking my power back was one of the most liberating and restorative things I have ever done

I did all of these and still it made no difference.

It was becoming a self-fulfilling prophecy. I believed I was going to fail. With each job I moved to, I would see the same things happening again and start to feel the same frustrations. It was like I was guiding my path in the same direction each time because I 'knew' what I expected to happen. And so it did.

It is too easy to give other people the power when your confidence is already dwindling and you feel lost. Too often we wait to be given permission to do things, put others first, wait until we are 'ready' or for a moment of clarity on the way forward. But we get this clarity and direction in giving ourselves the permission and by taking action. Taking my power back was one of the most liberating and restorative things I have ever done.

In the past, when I got to the point of flashing warning signs, I would start to look at roles elsewhere, which is why I ended up on a squiggly path. Other people would tell me I should work for myself, but it was difficult to see that as a way forward when my confidence had hit rock bottom. Add in the fear of losing all those promises of security and so on, and with a lifelong aversion to sales and phone calls, it was enough to put me off even thinking about it.

I let the stress go on way too long and these warning signs became panic attacks, anxiety, depression, arguments and huge uncontrollable emotions. They can, of course, take a long time to get over, and I fear some I may never move on from fully. I certainly have a few still hanging around that rear their heads every now and again. The telling change is that sometimes I now cry happy tears instead of just doom tears.

Anyone transitioning from employment to self-employment will have had some sign that things needed to change – a trigger or change of situation that finally made them leap.

Understanding your own triggers can help you look at areas where you may need to spend some time 'recovering' or dealing with emotions so that baggage doesn't weigh you down in your fabulous new life.

Even if you think your triggers and wobbles are behind you, now that you've left the job that was causing them, it is still helpful to reflect on your warning signs and how to deal with them.

You may need to keep an eye out for early warning signs in the projects you work on in self-employment too. If you start to feel on high alert, it can be a good indication that a client or project is not for you, and you can make changes. But it will not happen without you taking the time to reflect, assess your emotions and behaviours, and then taking some action. It is up to you to decide the severity of each of these and what you can take.

And trust your gut. It is usually right.

What are your warning signs?

....

....

....

....

....

Rate them out of 10 for their severity right now
(1 = low, 10 = high).

....

....

....

....

....

How would self-employment help you reduce
these scores?

....

....

....

....

....

STAGE THREE: HOPE AND DENIAL

This phase is where you keep telling yourself things will change. That a mystical day on the ever-moving horizon will bring magic and joy into your work. Others may even feed you hope, making you believe that something exciting is on the horizon.

You find yourself daydreaming. Hoping, wishing, longing for the day the magic comes.

You envision that miraculous day in the future when you feel more perky about getting up and dragging your more energetic carcass into work.

The day that you feel you are finally earning the wage you deserve for all your effort, shattered brain cells and fabulous ideas pulled out of your creative bank.

You will be progressing as you always dreamed, and it will be smooth running.

But this can also be like chasing the pot of gold at the end of the rainbow.

> "We are all naturally change-averse, so your logical mind will start generating logical arguments as to why starting later makes much better sense. In the end, these are all excuses. Your life is not going to be less busy later. You're not going to be better prepared later. Usually, the people who decide to wait just keep getting older and waiting longer."
> **Drew Rozell, *Write Like This, Not Like That*[2]**

In reality, we are fibbing to ourselves and getting stuck in a loop of hope and denial, where we convince ourselves (or others convince us) that something good will happen soon. The effort will pay off. You will be noticed (for good reasons). You go from one excuse to the next, justifying the letdowns. Some of the delusions I let myself believe were:

- This is just a phase.
- I'm just unlucky.
- If I could just get paid my worth.
- If I could just move desk.
- It's not that bad really! It could be worse.
- It will get better:
  ... when such and such leaves
  ... the nightmare student is removed
  ... after this project has ended
  ... maybe in the new financial year
  ... when they hire more staff
  ... when this nightmare client buggers off...
- <add your own options here>

This is how the employed world pulls you back when you start to consider a change and venture onto job boards. There is always a promise of something shiny just out of reach – a change, a promotion, a restructure, a new project, an extra responsibility. You believe it is a more secure career and has better benefits.

You can be stuck in this loop for years. Decades even. And when you see no other option, it is sometimes easier to just keep going, until it becomes increasingly hard to break the ties and get out.

In the United States, the 2017 SHRM Job Satisfaction report showed that only 29 per cent of employees are happy with career advancement opportunities.[3] And, here in the UK, a CIPD report recorded "a third (33 per cent) of UK employees say their career progression to date has failed to meet their expectations".[4]

And those figures are pre-pandemic, which has potentially changed the world of work for good. Many employees are now realising that there is a better way of working and want more from their employers and their work. Just 14 months into the never-ending fun of COVID, *Stylist* magazine's Women and Work survey confirmed "more than three quarters said their attitude to work is different from a year ago. The majority of women would like to work flexibly between home and office going forward. The major theme? As much as 81 per cent of women are now more focused on creating a better work-life balance".[5]

Many employees are now realising that there is a better way of working and want more from their employers and their work

However, in the current market, even full-time permanent roles are not very secure. "Now, we never know how long a new job is going to last. These days it is hard to find a working person who hasn't been laid off at least once. Some people have been laid off five or ten times."[6]

And as we saw in the previous chapter, many of the benefits have shrunk to be just a mere blurry reflection of what they used to be. Do you really want to sacrifice your happiness to stay in a job that makes you miserable just because it has a better pension (for now)?

I would start each new role with such hope and enthusiasm, then a year in, maybe two at most, the rose-tinted glasses would start to slide down my nose. I would get glimpses of reality. Until one day I'd wake up and feel defeated again.

I would stick it out a bit longer, before eventually being lured to the next shiny new role – for the cycle to start again.

I never stayed in any roles particularly long, and with each disappointment and dashed hope came an increasing feeling that I must be a failure. The last employed job was the longest position for me, at just three and a half years. There seemed to be nowhere I would fit.

Hope was rife. It ruled my days, guided my decisions, helped me pick myself back up. But relentless hope can only last so long when there are repeated disappointments. I started to feel like a mug for getting my hopes up. I had tried to force myself to fit where I was for way too long. What a mistake that was.

Then one day the hope was gone.

And I quit.

OVER TO YOU

For those who have not yet made the leap: Note and record your hope and denial thoughts over a two-week period. Are you trying to convince yourself things will change? Are you thinking false hopes or denying a problem exists?

How long have you been speaking this internal monologue? (This is a big indicator to show how long you have been struggling in the workplace.)

For the leapers: What did you use to tell yourself were the reasons you were staying in your employed role? How has this changed for you?

STAGE FOUR:
LIVING BY SOMEONE ELSE'S RULES

I've never been one for following the rules or the norms. I don't wear the latest fashions, possibly not even anything you could call fashion. We don't have a TV and both have an intense dislike of reality programmes, especially those along the lines of Love Island and Gogglebox. I have fairly unusual hobbies (archery, resin crafts, whittling, crocheting). I tend to have a serious dislike of books and films on the bestseller lists (yes, even *Harry Potter* and *The Lord of the Rings*). And, dare I admit, I am afraid of dogs and not a fan of cats. (How many of you have I just lost?)

It is not that I intentionally go out of my way to go against popular opinion, but more often than not I just don't get the fuss. If I don't like or agree with something, I don't see why a pretence is needed. I am much more comfortable not following the herd these days and standing up for my opinions.

However, that is not always ideal.

When working for someone else, you are obviously expected to live and work by their rules and the values that they dictate.

You sit where you're told, take lunch when you're told, sometimes even dress as you're told. You show up and leave when they say you can, take holidays when they allow. You work on the projects they tell you to. They tell you the ethos and values you should demonstrate and that have to matter to you. They tell you what websites you are allowed to visit and when you can use your phone. They decide on your pay, your progression, what meetings you are invited to. Sometimes you are even told when you can go to the loo.

That's a lot of terms being dictated to you.

Then there are the companies who like to give the appearance of you having your say, with annual surveys, team building days and staff development ... but in reality, so much of it is lip service and nothing ever comes from it. They know how to keep us quiet for a bit.

In essence, you can start to feel stripped of ... you. Your rights. Your freedom.

It strips you of flexibility, autonomy and the trust that you can be a grown-ass individual with the ability to decide how to work in the way that is best for you.

You can start to feel stripped of ... you. Your rights. Your freedom

When I look back, I can see how I felt like I was just a robot expected to turn up, function and leave. A cog in the soulless machine. And, certainly, to never upset the apple cart by questioning anything or taking my lunch 10 minutes early without begging furiously for forgiveness.

It becomes a game. One I lost in true dramatic style.

I couldn't keep up with the ever-changing rules. I am not sure I ever actually got the rule book in the first place, and certainly wasn't gaining any bonus points. I was not passing go and collecting £200. In fact, my wage often went down with a job change.

I was desperately trying to cling on to some sense of myself but being continually penalised for it. Every time I was dragged into a meeting room with "Can I have a word?", a bit more of me died inside.

> # HOW MUCH OF THIS WAS MY IDEA? DO I TRULY WANT ANY OF THIS, OR IS THIS WHAT I WAS CONDITIONED TO WANT? WHICH OF MY BELIEFS ARE OF MY OWN CREATION AND WHICH WERE PROGRAMMED INTO ME? HOW MUCH OF WHO I'VE BECOME IS INHERENT, AND HOW MUCH WAS JUST INHERITED? HOW MUCH OF THE WAY I LOOK AND SPEAK AND BEHAVE IS JUST HOW OTHER PEOPLE HAVE TRAINED ME TO LOOK AND SPEAK AND BEHAVE? WHO WAS I BEFORE I BECAME WHO THE WORLD TOLD ME TO BE?

GLENNON DOYLE, *UNTAMED*[7]

It was just before I went solo that I had a dawning realisation of how much damage had occurred in living by someone else's rules and the repeated failure to do so.

I was talented(ish), worked my backside off, and put in longer hours than most, but it all felt pointless. "I don't see the point any more" and "I don't know why I bother" became daily cries of frustrated despair.

Though opportunities kept getting dangled, they never materialised. I realised that I would never be getting any opportunities come my way as I was not malleable enough to be who they wanted me to be or an exact replica of management.

Finally, at some point I realised that a lot came down to company culture and values. And mine didn't align with theirs, or, as I now realise, with any corporate environment.

Though this is not a pleasant experience to go through, it can help you to determine what values you want to take forward into your own business. It can make you acutely aware of your priorities for yourself, your family and your future clients. It makes you realise what you stand for. And against.

I stand for allowing people to be themselves, creativity, honesty, being humble, grafting. Sharing ideas and skills – not keeping them to yourself in fear of someone stealing them or belittling you. Building a network of like-minded people, and forging relationships with clients who are on my wavelength.

I stand against the arrogance of many in the workplace, the backstabbing, the one-size-fits-all culture and the unpredictable environments where employees never quite know where they stand. The bullying, the micromanagement, the unethical behaviour. The taking credit of other people's work. The dampening of creativity and the fierce control over employees' careers.

I hated the robotic, emotionless stance that you had to have, particularly as a female in the workplace. Ironically, the more frustrated I got with this, the more emotional and stressed I became.

All this led to what I now recognise as the 'endless doom spiral': a desperation to prove I could do it. I could succeed. I tried anything and everything. But I tripped myself up at every turn.

It had a devastating effect on my self-confidence and mental health.

It resulted in me realising I was going to have to pretend to be someone else.

But I was no great pretender...

OVER TO YOU

Write down all the rules you can think of that you have to follow in your workplace (or a recent workplace if you have already left).

....
....
....
....

Looking at this list, how does it make you feel?

....
....
....
....

Where do they not align with how you want to work?

....
....
....
....

What values do you want to take forward into your business? (We will look at this more later, in part three.)

....
....
....
....

STAGE FIVE:
THE CONFUSED PRETENDER

When you get to the discombobulated state of confusion and loss of identity I was in, survival mode kicks in. For me, part of that meant some attempt at pretending to be this person I thought the employers wanted me to be.

I was even told to emulate the company 'darling' at one point, to put myself in her mind. To think, "What would she do?" in any given situation. While this darling was a lovely person and clearly on the fast track to success, we were very different people. We brought different skills, experiences and stories. This advice did nothing other than prove it was a one-size-did-all situation at the company. It didn't seem to even create a flicker of discomfort or recognition that this was not the fix for someone with chronic anxiety either – to basically tell someone they would not get anywhere if they didn't become someone else.

Aside from that rather startling issue, there were a number of other problems with this approach.

- I have always fled at even a mere mention of role play. It's no wonder I couldn't/didn't want to do this as that is what it essentially felt like: one long, never-ending role play.
- I clearly had no idea who the hell this fictional person was meant to be, or how to 'become' someone else.
- I also didn't personally know the darling that I was supposed to emulate. So, how was I to know what she would do in any situation?
- It is exhausting to keep up, and when starting from a position of already having chronic fatigue, this added to literally dragging myself through the day.
- It conflicted with my ingrained beliefs that you should be allowed to be yourself.

- There was so much hypocrisy and unpredictability in this suggestion. What was true for one person wasn't necessarily true for another. Why did I have to be a whole other person and others didn't?
- It is very difficult to get the inspiration to do your best work when you are having to spend what little energy reserves you have to get into character first.

I got so used to pretending and it went on so long I lost all sight of who I actually was. I even convinced myself I was an extrovert for crying out loud, in a bid to join in the company dos, activities and away days. I realise now how energy draining this whole experience was and how I utterly believed that I wanted to progress in that world. I saw no other way: I had to learn how to succeed. So, I kept trying.

I was even told to emulate the company 'darling' at one point, to put myself in her mind. To think, "What would she do?" in any given situation

Serious damage can be done when this goes on too long – to your identity, your mental health and your physical health. To your beliefs about yourself. To how you act around other people in your life too, not just at work. The world starts to look very bleak, odd and confusing.

And this was my experience in more than one company/organisation.

When I look back, I can see how I had to almost flick a switch in my head as I walked through the doors in the morning. But eventually all that expended energy caught up with me and I couldn't power it any longer. The mask slipped, the emotions came out and I felt so alone and frustrated. Nothing had worked. Not even another persona.

Without intending to sound all Jekyll and Hyde, I am a believer that you can sometimes slip into another person in your head to get you through something briefly. Like when people tell you to imagine your audience naked if you are terrified of public speaking. Maybe you could also slip into an alter ego or imagine you are some super-confident person you know to get you through the occasion.

Someone recently commented to me that in trying to teach online during the pandemic she "tried to harness her inner TV presenter". That sums it up perfectly. You can keep that up for a few hours or even a few days. But when it takes over all day every day, it is most definitely not sustainable.

When I look back, I can see that this started when I was diagnosed with a lifelong illness, one that can be very incapacitating. In one role, still reeling from being diagnosed with the illness, I was told by my manager, "Well, you can't do this job any more then", and was accused of having hidden this illness when I got the job three months earlier. In truth, I was informing her within 48 hours of actually getting the diagnosis and had gone into the office during my holidays specifically to tell her. I knew *something* was wrong but hadn't a clue what.

I kept going, and going, and going. Often until burnout, a meltdown or just utter exhaustion

A few years later, whilst I was employed by another company, I was again questioned over whether I was telling the truth and it was 'suggested' I pay privately to get a second opinion about the diagnosis as I "didn't look like I had it" … ignorance at its best. I'd had four neurologists by this point, so I think it was safe to say it was correct. I wasn't going to put myself through all that again.

Employment is supposed to be a safer bet for those with illnesses but what I, in fact, found was that it was making my condition worse. And when it is an 'invisible illness', it makes it all the more difficult to get others to understand.

So, I immediately went overboard trying to prove to myself and others that it was not going to get the better of me. And whenever I had to tell employers about it, I also had a point to prove to them too. No matter how much pain I was in or how I was struggling, I had to show it would not defeat me. I didn't want to be passed up for opportunities on the basis of an illness. (No matter how much companies shouldn't do this, we all know many do.) So, I kept going, and going, and going. Often until burnout, a meltdown or just utter exhaustion. It has become a habit so ingrained in me that I still battle with stopping and resting now.

The other thing that played a big role in pretending was comparisonitis. (We will look at this more in part three.) I was always comparing myself to and judging myself against others – their successes, their home life, their achievements, their clothes, their car ... and I always felt lacking.

Damn you, social media.

In the workplace this saw me comparing why others got opportunities that I didn't and unconsciously trying to pick up on their traits. Could I harness someone else's calm/language/social habits/effort level/work style? Would that help my cause?

Needless to say, it didn't.

One factor that I now realise had a huge impact on me was working in open-plan offices and classrooms. It can be quite crippling for someone with a huge dose of imposter syndrome and little confidence to know they are constantly being watched and assessed, all day every day, knowing that any minor infraction will be picked up on (possibly in front of the whole office). And if you are channelling your inner TV presenter/ darling of the workplace just to get through the day, then there is no space to be able to drop the front you are having to put on for even a moment.

Add in the fatigue, overstimulation (sounds and smells), paranoia, the unpredictability, competition, pressure to join cringeworthy team activities, temperature fluctuations and long commutes, and it was a hugely draining environment to be in for so much of my day.

So much had been stripped away. I had to do some serious work to find myself again

Ooooh, and the continual noise. I most definitely have misophonia. Noises that others can cope with can overwhelm me, break my brain, rile me up and create out-of-context reactions. Whistling, whispering, noisy eating and any kind of repetition, such as tapping and dogs barking, set me off. I also really struggle to block out sounds and conversations, so I found it incredibly hard to concentrate in an open-plan environment. (Don't get me started on working in schools.) Looking back, I now see how exhausting this was mentally and physically.

Offices, away days and team meetings are overwhelmingly designed for extroverts. If that is not you, it is a difficult place to be. It all added to my exhaustion and what was deemed my 'lack of resilience'. When you are falling asleep at the wheel of your car, you know it is time for things to change.

 Giles found this too. "I struggled with the noisy, open-plan offices with air conditioning that made it freezing in summer and boiling in winter, plus the whole traditional, inflexible nine to five regime and a commute on top."

After a couple of years, I started to realise this isn't me. I am not this person. And others started to comment on it too. I wasn't my usual self any more; my banter and humour had gone. My weight was fluctuating wildly with my moods, as I became obsessive about exercise and dieting, until I'd injure myself again and go back to comfort eating, physio and no exercise.

So much had been stripped away. I had to do some serious work to find myself again.

I gave up pretending and tried to go back to being me. But where the hell had I gone and how was I to get me back?

OVER TO YOU

Are you yourself at work? Does your business reflect the real you? If not, what stops you?

....

....

....

....

Or are you putting on a front? Why? What events have made you feel you need to do this?

....

....

....

....

How much do you think this affects your energy?

....

....

....

....

What changes could you make to get back to feeling like yourself?

....

....

....

....

STAGE SIX: BARGAINING … WAITING

Oh, those career gods up on the highest rung of the ladder … how I tried to bargain with them. Ask favours. Make them promises. Make bribes.

And I waited for their response … to no avail.

They either weren't listening or they were trying to tell me something (a little too subtly). So, I repeatedly bargained with myself.

"I'll give it another six months."

"I'll go for one more promotion."

"I will start putting my CV and portfolio together, then next time something rubbish happens it is ready to send out." Which became the 'next time', and the time after that.

I hear others bargaining with themselves in the same way.

"After Christmas."

"When the kids have gone off to college."

"When we've moved house."

But what are we waiting for? When we are at the point of making these bargains, we clearly know something is already wrong. It is like we almost have to wait for permission or for our thoughts and fears to be proved right yet again.

> "The plans remain as plans, unactioned, waiting for the perfect conditions to start."
> **Grace Marshall, *Struggle*[8]**

Though I have never been one for a firm career plan, instead going where the opportunities came up, I really just wasn't sure what else I should do. Where would I be happy? What company was finally going to be happy with little old creaky, clumsy, cranky me?

I had had my freelance design business on the side for about 10 years, but I had never had confidence in my graphics work and as a result just did really low-paid work for small local businesses. I was terrified to put myself out there or to ask for more than the token payments I was receiving. I certainly didn't see how I could make a full-time job out of the pittance I was earning and sporadic jobs I was getting in. It was just providing me with a bit of extra pocket money and spending money for holidays. I kept telling myself I needed to develop my skills and find my 'style' before I could fly solo.

Then there were the added doubts about being self-employed. The employed world and its cult-like status convinces you that working for yourself is not an option. There is no progress, no security, a hugely variable income, you have to do everything yourself, you don't have enough experience, you are not an 'entrepreneur', you have no business experience, you are crap at maths and so will mess up your accounts and get fined.

The corporate world and its cult-like status convince you that working for yourself is not an option

These doubts take root in your mind and you start to believe them. You stay (un)comfortably at your desk in the hideous open-plan office, often surrounded by people you would not socialise with through choice (apart from the few gems). You sacrifice yourself on the altar of the corporate gods.

You can get stuck here for years. I think I was severely bargaining for at least two years, and struggling for over a decade, before I fell off my rung for the last time. And I'm not alone.

- Matthew managed 18 years on the corporate treadmill feeling bullied, lifeless and depressed, suffering redundancies and stress, before he made the move.
- Giles looks back on 20 years and can see he was miserable for about 15 of those.
- Looking back on 15 years in employment, Craig says, "To be honest, I was unhappy at work most of the time back then."
- And Kate says, "Looking back, I can see that I struggled right from the start of working in that environment" but she pushed through 16 years in education and as a franchisee.
- Jo left her "bloody awful career" in teaching, to work in other areas of education and leadership for more than 10 years, where a good number of those years made her feel "nothing is enough".
- Sophie leapt from one "new challenge" to another, trying to find her place for seven years … but never found it.

It is only after three years of self-employment that I can now look back and see how long I had bargained with myself – pretty much my whole career until the leap. I was clearly just not meant for the world of employment.

I still have to deal with bargaining in my business now – mostly potential clients trying to knock my prices down or asking me to complete work to tighter schedules – but as with other negatives, I am in control now. It is my choice to accept the bargaining or refuse. To work late and charge an extra fee for the privilege, or just suck it up. To take on work out of my comfort zone and 'work it out later', or stick to the stuff I know about and have an easier life. That control alone hugely changes the dynamics.

And I still bargain with myself – but mostly over more joyous things, such as, yes, you can register on another bloody course – when you have finished AT LEAST one of the 17 you have in progress.

I have a tough boss.

OVER TO YOU

What are you counting on coming to pass that is holding you back? Is it a true issue or an excuse you are making due to fear of the unknown?

....
....
....
....
....
....

Have you set a repeatedly moving deadline for something you want to achieve?

....
....
....
....
....
....

How can you reframe this to mean you can take action and pursue what you want?

....
....
....
....
....
....

STAGE SEVEN: A BROKEN SYSTEM

By the time you have worked through all the previous stages, it is quite easy to see why for many the world of employment is a broken system. It just doesn't work for them. It comes as no surprise at this point that I was one of them.

In working for others, you find yourself in a workplace eco-system which can be exclusive, damaging and elitist. But also out-of-date, unprofessional, corrupt, and quite frankly disturbing.

Toxic, unhealthy workplaces are rife in the employment world. These are the very essence of one-size-fits-all and backstabbing. Unhealthy competition is encouraged. Employees feel unsupported, stunted in their growth and struggle for opportunities. There is little logical behaviour. Some staff are made to feel a failure for daring to breathe the wrong way, while others can get away with murder.

This isn't to say all businesses are toxic nightmares, though my personal experience suggests otherwise. My time spent in education alone had levels of toxicity that were so ingrained I can never see the culture going back to toxic-free. (See Jo and Kate's stories for tales of education too.)

When you look at conversations between freelancers and the self-employed, there is an overwhelming commonality of having experienced sexist, racist, toxic workplaces. There is something about us as a community that just didn't stand for that crap. When you spend so much of your life

When you spend so much of your life at work, it is only fair that you should feel happy, or at least comfortable there

at work, it is only fair that you should feel happy, or at least comfortable there.

Sadly, if you are a person with morals, values and a sense of justice, toxic workplaces become a very frustrating and stressful place to be. Because they won't change. It is you who is expected to change. You can fight all you like, but you are shouting into a void. And the less I was heard, the more wound up I got, the more I fought, and the more it came back at me.

The amazing thing with toxic workplaces is the lack of realisation from management as to what is going on at lower levels, even though staff turnover rates are soaring. The bullying, snide comments, lack of flexibility, favouritism, promotions given on the sly, and underhand tactics at taking credit for others' work appear to fly underneath the radar. Not to mention the old-fashioned approach to working that is still steadfastly being adhered to in many organisations, which doesn't reflect the needs of this next generation of workforce.

Difficulties are often instead attributed to others; at the moment, the favourite being the 'flakiness and diva demands of millennials'. As millennials now make up 50 per cent of the global workforce, maybe they should be taken more seriously.

IT'S CLEAR THAT MILLENNIALS WILL BE A POWERFUL GENERATION OF WORKERS AND THAT THOSE WITH THE RIGHT SKILLS WILL BE IN HIGH DEMAND. THEY MAY BE ABLE TO COMMAND NOT ONLY CREATIVE REWARD PACKAGES BY TODAY'S STANDARDS, BUT ALSO INFLUENCE THE WAY THEY WORK AND WHERE AND HOW THEY OPERATE IN THE WORKPLACE. THEY MAY ALSO REPRESENT ONE OF THE BIGGEST CHALLENGES THAT MANY ORGANISATIONS WILL FACE.

PWC, "MILLENIALS AT WORK: RESHAPING THE WORKPLACE"[9]

Those deemed to be resilient can often work through these challenges, and the 'chosen few' fly through with barely a hair out of place or wobble in the slightest. But for those who care about their work, who take heart in what others say about them (good or bad) and who have actual beating human hearts, this type of atmosphere can be devastating. It can significantly affect mental health and have lasting damage.

The defining moment comes when you realise that it is the workplace culture that is flawed, not you.

Let me just pause here while we reflect on that...

IT IS THE WORKPLACE CULTURE THAT IS FLAWED, NOT YOU.

It may be a while before you do fully believe this. It took me a good 18 months or so after entering self-employment. Though I kind of thought it somewhere in the recesses of my mind, when you are doubting every inch of your sanity and beliefs, you start to believe what people tell you.

The defining moment comes when you realise it is the workplace culture that is flawed, not you

To believe that, in fact, it wasn't that I was a hideous person, or unable to do my job due to my disability, or lack of skill, or that I wasn't resilient enough. Working for others is just not for me. It has taken me a long time to be able to say, and understand, that.

I need flexibility, control, a peaceful space to work and the freedom to be creative and articulate myself. Not to be shoved in a box and silenced. Not to be restrained from the self-development and continued learning I love so much. Not to have to beg for opportunities and time to develop. I certainly never understood why creative companies would dampen the creativeness of the individuals it hired for that very purpose.

Don't look at your experiences in the workplace as a reflection of you, your skills and your personality. Look back at how the environment changed and what led to the toxicity, and how you have/had no control in this.

Identify it for what it is – a broken system, not a broken you.

OVER TO YOU

If you have experienced a toxic workplace, think about
what beliefs you hold from that experience – beliefs
that are not true, even if you currently believe they may
be. Identify the experiences that have damaged your
confidence and opinion of yourself.

....

....

....

....

....

Then think about what you value, what you want to
change, what thought patterns you may need to confront.

....

....

....

....

....

....

"

SOMETIMES I WAKE UP
AND HAVE TO REMIND
MYSELF: 'THERE IS NOTHING
WRONG WITH ME. I HAVE
PATTERNS TO UNLEARN, NEW
BEHAVIOURS TO EMBODY
AND WOUNDS TO HEAL. BUT
THERE IS NOTHING WRONG
WITH THE CORE OF ME AND
WHO I AM. I AM UNLEARNING
GENERATIONS OF HARM AND
REMEMBERING LOVE. IT
TAKES TIME.

YOLO AKILI[10]

PART 2

MAKING THE LEAP. LANDING THE FALL.

Possibly the scariest part of the process of launching into self-employment is finally making the decision and taking action. Moving past the fears that are holding you back and keeping your feet firmly planted where you are not happy. Handing in your resignation. Making those first giant steps.

"One small step for man…" – Neil Armstrong hasn't got a clue.

More like "One mahoosive terrifying leap for (wo)man…"

Instead of letting fear win, celebrate the alarm going off in your brain. Cliché incoming through – Today is a new day!

You no longer need to stay in this place where you are uncomfortable and anxious. You no longer need to feel pushed down, insignificant or a failure. You no longer have to make chit-chat around the scaly staff kettle or grimace your way through team building activities and away days. You no longer have to stand on a stage and clap while people dressed as dancing peas sashay by. (True story. My poor sister – the resentful clapper, not the dancing pea.)

It may take you time to make a plan and get out, but just knowing the plan is there should give you a little bounce back in your bunny hop

It may take you time to make a plan and get out, but just knowing the plan is there should give you a little bounce back in your bunny hop. To know you have an escape. That there is a better life for you on the horizon whether immediately or in the near future.

In this section we look at the emotions that are likely to appear during and after making the leap, and how to ride them.

In *Struggle,*[11] Grace Marshall defines these phases of recognition, reckoning and revelation as:

- Oh shit...
- What is this shit?
- Holy shit!

We've covered Oh shit... in part one. You have realised that things are not working for you. You realised something needed to change and that you were going to have to take action.

Now you get to ask, What is this shit?, as you start to redefine expectations, your story and your future. Then you can really fly while screaming Holy shit! from the rooftops.

Here's our journey through part two, to help you in your reckoning.

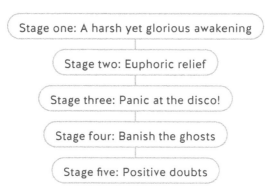

Stage one: A harsh yet glorious awakening

Stage two: Euphoric relief

Stage three: Panic at the disco!

Stage four: Banish the ghosts

Stage five: Positive doubts

If there was any kind of logical sequence in emotions, this is how I envisage it would look. However, not everyone's journey will follow all the steps, or in a given order, and each of us will find different phases more challenging than others. Some people may work through them all, while others may jump straight to stage five. Some may celebrate first, then later be bombarded with doubts and panic. My route through was definitely a discombobulated squiggle.

We all have our own journey to make. By being aware of where we have come from, how far we have come and what lies ahead, we can begin to smash, or at least squash, a few bumps in the road.

Some of you might already have made the leap, and if you have, there is still purpose in taking the time to reflect on your journey, moving past and healing any areas that may still be causing you issues or upset. You might actually be in a better place to process some things now. I know I certainly am.

We all have our own journey to make

This is the shortest of the sections as the actual fall is not where we want to linger any longer than we have to. The word 'fall' may not do it justice as this is, in fact, a powerfully positive step, more of a joyous leap. Once you have made the decision, you are likely to want to crack on. Either way, there is true purpose in making sure you take in your experiences and use them to fuel you to a successful career in self-employment and to define what truly matters to you.

A HARSH YET GLORIOUS AWAKENING

I'm not sure there was one moment for me. There were many, chipping away at me piece by piece, eroding my sanity, confidence and stability for a long time.

There was an increased awareness with each instance that something wasn't right, that this wasn't how things should be. Eventually came the dawning slap across the face with the cold hand of reality. I realised how toxic a place I had ended up in.

There were times when someone really should have had my back and didn't.

And times where an apology should have been made. But I seemed to be the only one expected to apologise.

Admittedly, I had been here before, but this time was different. It was on another level altogether. No sideways move into yet another company was going to pick me up this time or fix the damage done. I had to get out.

I had to get out for the sake of my health. Not just out of that job, but out of employed life. Away from working for others and the oppressive environments in which I clearly didn't fit.

It was an awakening.

Light switch on.

It is the moment where you realise nothing will change. That all expectations are on you to be the one to change. Maybe that you have hit rock bottom and the only way is up, which won't happen while working for others. There is a better option out there, and you have the skills to go for it, to work for yourself. You just need to orientate yourself and find which way is up.

If you haven't had your glorious awakening yet, given that you are reading this book, I suspect it may be on its way.

Once you have it, there is no going back. For most of us anyway.

You can spend years debating the options and wanting to leave, but the moment that decision is made and lodged in your mind something cataclysmic shifts.

You cannot shake the significance of knowing that everything is fundamentally wrong. Reality has infiltrated your brain and you know there is a better way.

This is your wake-up call.

You finally realise what is happening. You know what you need to do.

You don't fit the mould – and you finally realise that's okay.

You may have had that moment of "Oh! It might not be me after all. Others feel like this too" or "This just isn't a good fit for me".

You can see it for the broken system it is.

So, why do we hold out for so long?

Why do we chain ourselves to the job?

I recently heard someone talk about this (and I cannot for the life of me remember who or where – apologies to that person) – not just chaining ourselves to the job, but the status or title that comes with it. You can be chained to the wage, or to a specific title, whether that is director or manager, or just your actual role.

You may feel that because you have trained in a certain subject and spent a fortune on a degree in it, that you have to stay there. Even if it is making you feel absolutely miserable or you realise there is another job or industry you now feel more love for. I know I felt that for a long time.

Add in the eroding confidence, the burning shame and embarrassment at having 'failed' in your job, and the stubbornness that you have to make it work, and you can easily tell yourself that you are justified in staying put.

> *You may feel that because you have trained in a certain subject and spent a fortune on a degree in it, that you have to stay there*

When I was at my lowest point, just before going solo, I felt like I had totally wasted the six years I had spent in higher education; the time I had spent training and retraining in all the directions my squiggly career had gone, and that I had wasted a fortune as a result. I couldn't see a way out, and certainly didn't see how all my many and varied experiences would come together. I definitely didn't see how I would ever be happy in work. I had worked in so many places, and though I had made some great friends in my colleagues, I never quite seemed to get management on my side, and I ended up trusting no one.

I got to the point where I thought, I'm in my mid-30s, I've failed at everything so far, I have wasted so much time and money. I just HAVE to make this work. So, I pushed on, and on. Past my sanity limits, turned left at my health limits. Stuck on a roundabout to nowhere in never-ending circles.

Though I often say I kind of fell into self-employment, this is actually a reflection of me playing it down. If it wasn't for all the experiences I had gained and the many skills I had picked up along the way, my business would not be thriving as much as it is. It had actually taken over a decade trying to find my feet. The 'overnight success' of the business was a long time in the making. Without realising it, I had actually amassed a wealth of experiences and skills which aligned fantastically, once I found the right path for me.

The current Western education system forces us to make decisions about our careers from a very young age. We choose exam subjects from 13 or 14 years old and are then expected to stick with them – as if we all know, as teenagers establishing our identities, what we want to be doing for the rest of our lives. Some people do grow up knowing exactly what they want to be, and I applaud that, but most of us don't. Plus, at that age you don't even know a fraction of the jobs that exist out there. Many of the jobs the next generation will do don't yet exist.

IN MANY INDUSTRIES AND COUNTRIES, THE MOST IN-DEMAND OCCUPATIONS OR SPECIALTIES DID NOT EXIST 10 OR EVEN FIVE YEARS AGO, AND THE PACE OF CHANGE IS SET TO ACCELERATE. BY ONE POPULAR ESTIMATE, 65 PERCENT OF CHILDREN ENTERING PRIMARY SCHOOL TODAY WILL ULTIMATELY END UP WORKING IN COMPLETELY NEW JOB TYPES THAT DON'T YET EXIST.

WORLD ECONOMIC FORUM[12]

If this is the case, how can we possibly expect to stay in a career for life that we potentially chose when we were 13? Times have changed – and continue to change – at a pace that is unfathomable. Gone are the days of leaving school, starting a job and staying in that company for many years, if not until retirement. Many of us currently at a working age had parents who did that exact thing, so we can often feel an expectation (or burden) that we should do the same. Our parents' generation may even expect this.

You are allowed to say bye to something that no longer gives fire in your belly

I am lucky that although my parents both stayed in a career for life, they were enthusiastic about my many wanderings. It probably helps that I was always filled with gusto for the next challenge but fair play to them, they never had words with me about it all. My mum did warn me about teaching … maybe I should've listened to that one (although I would not be in eLearning now if I had, so something good has come out of that particular catastrophe).

The more jobs you undertake, the more you find out about different roles, try out new things, and learn new skills and industries. If one of them particularly takes your fancy or you discover you are good at something new, why the hell shouldn't you pursue it? That is not a failure. I'd hesitate to even call it a blip. You are allowed to find new passions. In fact, it should be celebrated. It is a benefit of the modern world of work that opportunities to retrain are easier to come by and more affordable, and you are allowed to say bye to something that no longer gives fire in your belly. Just as you serve in your job, your job has to serve you.

I had never heard of an instructional designer until I became one. It was a total accident, but what a happy one it was. Eventually. And it was the same with content design – I had never heard of this as a discipline. It is only because of a previous, and misleading, job title I'd had (I was actually a graphic designer/illustrator) that someone contacted me about what was to become my first self-employed contract in this new world.

In essence, what I am saying is do not attach your worth to a job title, a wage, regrets over wasted time/money, and certainly not to a (often imagined) guilt trip. Embrace the wake-up call, and believe your worth.

I'd love to hear where it takes you.

OVER TO YOU

What beliefs do you hold about your job/industry? If you are unhappy in your job, why do you feel you need to stay there?

....

....

....

....

....

....

Have you had **the** moment? Have you acted on it? If so, how did it feel? If not, what is holding you back?

....

....

....

....

....

....

What would you love to do? Could you start taking some steps to working towards that as a goal?

....

....

....

....

....

....

EUPHORIC RELIEF

I remember sitting on the settee in the kitchen just staring out the patio doors ... and smiling.

For the first time in months.

My chest was fluttery with excitement and nerves. The fog in my head cleared with the relief and was replaced with a sense of calm. It felt like a boulder had been lifted off my shoulders, that I could breathe again. I felt a sense of joy that had been missing for a long time. I no longer had to sit on the edge of the bed in tears every morning, fearing of what the day would bring. I didn't have to spend every day having panic attacks in the staff toilets. I didn't have to feel guilty for going to physio. I didn't have to use my last ounce of energy and brain power to make conversation with someone who was making life very difficult for me.

I had no plan but anything had to be better than the situation in which I'd found myself

There were tears of relief rather than panic.

Why?

I had done it. I had handed my notice in.

I was going to be my own boss. I was in control. I could work to my own terms.

I had no plan but anything had to be better than the situation in which I'd found myself.

Matthew experienced similar. "My wife said when I left that job in 2010, a weight lifted. I didn't show up at her house looking sad and beaten at the end of the week. I smiled and was just really happy."

It cannot be underestimated how much of a life changer that moment is.

Euphoria may have come as an instant hit to you when you handed your notice in, as it did for me. Or maybe it was more of a slow burner.

It may even take some time to hit. But when it does, sit with it. Don't be afraid to celebrate it. You've made a big step.

The feeling may be different for you depending on the circumstances in which you are leaving. You might not class it as euphoria. Maybe it is relief, excitement and clarity (bundled in with nerves and a bit of fear no doubt), knowing you are making a positive move.

Sometimes it just becomes clear it is the right time.

"If I was that integral to someone else's business, imagine what I could do for my own!" – Jo

When Jo went solo she was leaving a job in which she had actually been quite happy, but it had become clear there was little chance of progression or a wage rise. When I asked Jo how it felt to hand in her notice she said, "It felt great – like the right time and a positive move. My boss tried to get me to stay (which was really nice), yet he still apparently couldn't offer more money, which I felt would have been the mark of respect and value I deserved. So, I asked for my wage to stay the same, but for my hours to decrease to give me time to develop (and earn from) agoodwriteup. My boss said he needed me full time as I was integral to the business ... but I felt that if I was that integral to someone *else's* business, imagine what I could do for my own!"

That is one heck of a defining moment, when you realise that all that effort you are putting in for someone else could actually be being used for your own business. Your own development. Your own profit. To build something all of your own.

Though that can feel terrifying, risky and overwhelming, there is likely to be a barrage of positive emotions too. Focus on those.

How does it feel for you?

Write it down. Let it sink in. Believe that you can do this.

Mark the occasion and celebrate it annually. Or more frequently if you wish. The rules are yours to set now.

Most of all, your task is to sit and enjoy it.

Maybe even partake in some fizz. If ever there was a reason to, this is it. Maybe even for breakfast.

OVER TO YOU

Note down how this moment feels. You may want to come back to this as a reminder when panic or doubts creep in. Or if you have a bad day and a wobble. You could even share it on social media. This can be your first step into being authentic and sharing your experiences, which we will look at in part three.

....

....

....

....

....

....

PANIC AT THE DISCO!

Once the euphoria had settled, the fear and stark reality took over.

"What the hell am I going to do now?"

I had no plan. No idea where to even start. At all. With the state of my mind, I had not applied for roles, sourced clients or got my portfolio prepared. I had not had the headspace to rationally think it through. I hadn't even emptied my desk drawers back in the office.

So, I had my usual reaction and launched into action. I dug out my portfolio files and CV. I had a look at my (at the time) crappy out-of-date website and started to form one of my beloved to-do lists. The thought that kept me powering through was "anything has to be better than this".

The world was my clichéd oyster. But that was terrifying.

Along came a new type of panic.

The removal of a panic associated with the very real, daily threat of being in a toxic ecosystem where I didn't fit in made way for a whole new type of panic – a panic caused by the fear of the unknown, of the potential difficulties that could surely appear again in the next job. The unknown of where my next wage was going to come from.

When you are in the depths of stress, it is hard to see that the next place will be any different, or that there is a way out. That there is a place where you can be happy. Or at least content.

It takes quite a lot of awareness to rein yourself in at this point. To realise that you have gone to What If Land. You are transferring a real threat onto a very unreal one. You are catastrophising about the future when you have no idea how that is even going to be shaped yet.

Panic can be further compounded by the feeling of being pushed, being made redundant or sacked, a temporary contract coming to an end or any other additional stressors. Maybe there are or were unresolvable differences that make you feel there is no alternative. Or maybe there are fears about providing for your family, or paying your mortgage. Possibly a feeling of letting somebody (or, sometimes even worse, yourself) down. Maybe there's a health issue that is difficult to manage and you have fears of how future employers or clients will deal with it.

There are different types of panic. Some will come and go easier than others

Either way, it is important to recognise that there are different types of panic. Some will come and go easier than others and some will be here to stay thanks to our inbuilt fight or flight response and caveman instincts.

Given the scale of panic attacks I was having, maybe I am not the person to give you any advice about how to deal with this chapter of your life, and I would certainly advise getting the help of a professional. But then again, I have certainly had a lot of practice and now I have come through the other side, I can see some things that may have helped me.

I am no therapist, so I will not go into the 'fixes' for panic, or down the CBT lane (which has helped me in looking at my personal triggers – catastrophiser and black and white thinker coming through), but let's look at why you might be panicking. If you can understand this, it helps to make great strides in moving forward.

There are three main triggers for panic that I have seen, and experienced, in the workplace.

- The unknown – Usually something out of your control, these are the things that creep up on you and come out of left field. For example, being made redundant or an unexpected problem with a project landing on your shoulders. Also included here are those things that are hoisted on you in an office environment and pre-indicated by "Can I have a word?" or "Why do you think you have been brought into this meeting?" from your manager, when you likely have no idea what it's about.
- The hypothetical – There are events that you imagine, that have not been shown to be true (yet at least). They can, however, feel very real, particularly when in the throes of anxiety. When experiencing this trigger, you are often told you are being paranoid, pessimistic or overreacting (which at least provides some validity when it turns out you were right to be worried). These thought patterns are often along the lines of "If I do X, then Y will happen", even though there is no evidence to prove this.
- The known – These are the real threats that have already been shown to be true and continue to be an issue. Or where you know you have gone wrong. However unintentional, maybe you did cock something up. Maybe you did say something that you know you shouldn't. Or maybe it is something unwarranted but you know it is still going to come and bite you on the butt, as it has done before.

Regardless of how you decided to leap into self-employment, the panic you are facing in this case is likely to be significantly about the unknown. You can't possibly know how the next few months are going to pan out. You can just try your damn hardest to make it a good one. This is fuelled by the hypothetical questions we ask ourselves. What if I don't find any clients? What if the business fails? What if I don't earn enough? Did I do the right thing?

Each of these triggers creates stress and fear, particularly when it occurs suddenly or the consequences are unknown. And they can be short term or long term. They are all valid responses.

However, each trigger needs to be dealt with differently, so the first step is to reflect on which of these types of panic you are experiencing so that you can understand it a little better. Then ask yourself – are the consequences likely to be as bad as you are imagining, or are you catastrophising?

If we can learn to use it wisely, panic can also fire us into action

Consider where you can get some reassurance when you start to panic – a loved one, friend, family or online network who can talk you down from it and help you see through the fog. I have found online networks particularly helpful for this as if you find the right tribe (we will come onto this), they just get you. They understand your fears, however daft you may think they are. Or how serious.

We have to be careful with hypothetical panic, in particular, as it can become a self-fulfilling prophecy. If you worry about something 'imagined' for long enough, you can unwittingly push yourself down that path. I have got the T-shirt on that one. This phenomenon is known as the Pygmalion effect – when high expectations can lead to better performance, and low expectations can lead to worse performance.

Also, consider that a panic that is currently hypothetical could also become a known panic down the line. Or an unknown which happens repeatedly could also become known. Similarly, after a known panic, we may worry over and over that it will happen again, and it becomes hypothetical.

If we can learn to use it wisely, panic can also fire us into action. It can make us do things we may have been procrastinating about for ages. It can make us try new things, to develop ourselves. We have to find ways to make it a positive experience. To gain something we want.

It can help us make that decision to leap.

Hopefully your panic will bugger off and lead to a period of calm and clarity, and you can start to process the causes, which is where you will start to move into acceptance.

What kind of panic are you experiencing? Is it real or
hypothetical?

....
....
....
....
....
....

Is what is in your head worse than what you were
experiencing when working for others?

....
....
....
....
....
....

When you start to panic, list all the things that are better
already (or will be when you make the leap), such as no
commute, flexible hours, working from home, and so on.

....
....
....
....
....

BANISH THE GHOSTS

Once you have moved past the fear and panic, you can start to accept where you are and what you need to do to make changes. To accept what you need to do to embrace the new challenge of self-employment.

I was letting past experiences hold me back, and in that way, I was still handing my control over to others

You may not be happy about the situation. You may feel hurt, confused, angry and lost. But don't let that stop you accepting the situation, because only then can you move forward.

This was a huge learning curve for me, and one I only discovered a year or so into self-employment. I was letting past experiences hold me back, and in that way, I was still handing my control over to others. I was letting my worries about what previous colleagues and employers thought stop me from being visible. I was holding back from fully engaging in the industry communities as old colleagues would be there. I was still battling to move on from their judgement, when in reality they had probably long since forgotten about me or stopped caring, as companies do once you move on.

Once I accepted that what had happened had happened, and the only thing I could do now was to concentrate on myself – to get better, develop my skills and establish the business – it led to a significant change in my mindset.

If I was going to stay working in the same industry, I was going to have to move on.

Banish the ghosts.

What can we learn from this?

You may be euphoric at the leap you have taken, but you still need to ground yourself and put a plan into action.

Accept that things are going to change.

Accept that you may have to make sacrifices to take steps forward.

Accept that you are now in control!

Accept that you need to prioritise YOU.

Accept that you will take time to heal.

Accept that things will not always go your way.

Accept that there will still be ups and downs ahead.

Accept that things may never be the same again. (Halle-flipping-lujah!)

Accept that only you can do this.

Accept that there may be ghosts of your past loitering, but how you deal with them now will speak volumes about you as a person.

Just don't accept any more crap.

By accepting, you are also acknowledging that:

- Change is good.
- You are in control.
- You are a priority.
- You have power.
- You know the road ahead may be long, but it will be so much better.

- You can deal with whatever life throws at you.
- You will not allow things to continue as they were.

I feel I have gone a bit Oprah here. Maybe I was harnessing that all along.

This may seem like a daunting set of things to accept right now, but bank them in your mind. Work on them one at a time if you need to. Just don't let them slide into the dark recesses of your mind never to think about again. Start to believe them.

Through these steps you can start to forge a plan of action, both for building your business, and for rebuilding yourself.

Write down all the things you accept relating to your current situation. If you are struggling, use the list above, but change them into 'I accept...' statements.

Stick this list up by your desk, or at least have it handy. When having a wobble, read it, say it aloud. Chant it to yourself like a mantra. Let the words sink in, and take time to reflect on how close you are to believing these statements.

Which do you need more time and help to work towards? What plans can you put in place to address them?

POSITIVE DOUBTS

Just as the relief and the panic may cause conflict in your brain, you may also wildly veer between acceptance and doubt.

Doubts show you care, have awareness. That you are realistic and have a critical mind. That you are leaping in with your eyes open. It is when you let them take control that they become a problem.

I haven't come across a freelancer yet who doesn't suffer from bouts of imposter syndrome, self-doubt and feelings of inadequacy. But this reflects them wanting to deliver their best, to make the best of everything, and maybe being (a tiny bit) self-critical.

I never got the "Oh my, what have I done?" feelings after the leap, but I know many do. And not just at the start of their journey. There is many a cry of "Is it even worth it?" after being screwed over by a client or dealing with a shitty customer. We are human. We doubt many a smaller decision, so of course you will sometimes doubt a decision of this scale.

Even once the business is off the ground and ticking along, some people still feel the call to go back to the other side – and that's okay. They obviously had a better experience in employment than I, and many others, did – or they have short memories. If you have a great experience working for a particular client and they offer a permanent role, it can be very tempting.

So, where do the doubts come from?

It is a daunting prospect to suddenly know you are in charge and that everything is down to you. You are responsible for accounts, tax returns, marketing, project management, scheduling, pitching, sales – and everything else. On top of the actual client work.

Craig echoes this in his interview. "Self-employment has been more hard work than I expected; the added hassle of dealing with your website, accounts, insurance, pension and all that takes up time. But I'd rather not go back to employed life."

I agree – but how powerful is it having this level of control?

I have found that I actually enjoy some of the aspects of the business that I didn't think I would, and have found ways to help my motivation, such as belonging to accountability groups and joining networks where we work together.

There are ways to get help with those parts of running a business that you don't like or are less confident with. I am absolutely useless with numbers and terrible with money, so having an accountant was always the first priority for me. After a few months I also enlisted a financial adviser (yes, I know – pretentious much?) to help me sort all the pension shenanigans as, again, I don't have a clue.

Use the doubts to create positive action for yourself

Three years on I realise how much I HATE WordPress, so I have enlisted help with that too. It is much more cost-effective to pay someone else to look at this for me than to lose hours amending (read: breaking) things, only to have to fix them again or give up and leave them broken. There are crazy loons out there who love WordPress, so let them have it.

Many have a fear of enlisting such help due to the costs involved. But these guys and gals do in an hour what would take me a full day, at least, and so by being free to work on client projects at that time, I am earning more than I am paying out. Win–win.

What's the best way to deal with your doubts?

Prepare yourself for these moments. Recognise when they appear and have a plan for dealing with them. Sit with them for a while. Don't jump to a response.

Use the doubts to create positive action for yourself – by networking, talking to connections, sharing experiences, getting help. It can even make great social media content!

Make time to talk to fellow freelancers and business owners. You will soon find they have had exactly the same doubts and may have some nuggets of wisdom for you. And if not, they will certainly have words of encouragement and you will feel less alone. I have found the freelance communities to be the biggest source of support I have had, except for my chap and family. There is always someone there to answer your questions, share your fears and ambitions, fight your corner, point you in the direction of helpful resources or, as I often request, tell you a crap joke. But remember to make sure you respond to the queries of others too and build regular engagement. Don't let it be one-sided.

There are a number of networks for all manner of industries, but some of those I use most regularly are detailed in the recommended resources section at the back of this book.

Now, there's only one thing for it – let's see what the future can look like for you, and how you can get there.

What doubts do you have about working for yourself?
How are you going to deal with them?

....
....
....
....
....
....

Which networks are you going to join (and engage in) so
you have support when you need it?

....
....
....
....
....
....

Identify the tasks you struggle with and look at costs for
getting help. What would this save you in lost project time?
Weigh up the balance and see if it is worthwhile for you.

....
....
....
....
....
....

PART 3

NEW ASCENT. NEW RULES.

Now we leave the crappy experiences behind, using them as nothing more than a tool to push you forward. You can tear up the rule book that has controlled your life so far and start to rewrite it your own way.

We can all take a leaf out of Matthew's approach. "The way I see it, those experiences got me to where I am today. It took me eight years from leaving that toxic workplace to work for myself, but it was worth the wait."

It can be very daunting to think about restarting. It feels huge. Overwhelming in fact. You are likely to still be feeling a huge range of emotions, from anger, fear, bitterness and confusion, to joy, happiness, relief and excitement. And everything in between. But remember that you are still using your years of experience; you are just going down a new route. One that is not going to be dictated to you.

Sure, there will be moments where you feel lost; tough days and battles to be had. But they will be *your* battles. *You* will have control (mostly). *You* will be making the decisions.

It is such a satisfying feeling when you move on from tough experiences to finally be able to show how you have turned things around, how you are flying on your own. For ex-colleagues to see amazing feedback from your clients (and even some of their competitors) and to see your face pop up in lots of places, to be heavily involved in various areas of the industry and to be asked to speak at events, be on podcasts and to win awards.

It allows you to move on physically and mentally, to get rid of the demons that still haunt you, and to finally see your achievements and successes for yourself. And to show the world them too.

Even if you left your corporate job with a happy skip and fond memories, you may need to deal with a sense of loss. Especially if you were a victim of redundancy or a pandemic throwing the world upside down. Or if you fell into it by accident. Isn't it still a wonderful feeling to succeed on your own and something you want to celebrate? To show you are a capable human being, that there is a path out there which is perfect for you, that you created.

> *We all have shitty days. Don't let them knock you back down. Learn from the situation, reflect, move on*

While you can deal with such emotions when starting out on your next step, recognising and dealing with them as early as possible can help prevent you carrying them on into your next venture (as I did initially) or at least help to diminish their ongoing impact. As I mentioned in the introduction, in my first contract role, I let my fragile state affect relationships and I hid away from the expert status with which I was labelled. If I had been more aware of how to handle the emotions and baggage I was carrying into the role, been more open and asked for help, it would have been much smoother sailing.

It is in part three that you will see the most progress, and hopefully (cheese coming through) find yourself.

You will need to reprogramme your brain and your beliefs about yourself. You will have wobbles, and oh, how you will need to establish boundaries – I am still looking for those damn elusive things a lot of the time. But all this is doable, and in this section we are going to look at this, and much more.

Sometimes you may feel you take one step forward to take three back, but it is all part of your development. We all have shitty days. Don't let them knock you back down. Learn from the situation, reflect, move on.

And, most importantly, document your journey so you can look back and see how far you have come. Some ideas for how to do this coming up!

In the words of the freelance queen herself, Sophie Cross:

> "I think finding your voice and knowing what you're best at can take a long time and is an ongoing journey. If you see it as that instead of having to make the perfect decision and sticking to it, then it becomes a lot easier. Everything can and will change. Change is the only constant and I take comfort from change."

Let's embrace the changes to come.

Take it one step at a time, and enjoy.

THOSE FIZZY FEELINGS

The first thing I want you to do is to celebrate, however that looks for you – drowning yourself in a vat of fizz, shoving your face in a box of fancy chocolates, a dance around the kitchen, a brew and a biscuit, shouting a large "SCREW YOU" from the rooftops.

Take time to reflect on the huge step you have taken. Let it sink in. Bask in your glory. Take a deep breath.

Feels good, doesn't it?

Before we get to the real action, I want to share some tips for how I have celebrated moments throughout the last three years as these will be a great way for you to record your journey as you go it alone.

If you can get into the habit of using some or all of these, it will help you to track your progress, identify your personal and professional development, celebrate milestones and also provide you with great social media content.

Here they are, the five tools in my celebration toolkit.

Little book of epic wins

This is a small notebook that sits on my desk. I record all achievements no matter how big or small. It is a great tool to flick back through and remind yourself of lots of fantastic highs.

I just doodle and scribble things down in coloured pens (I treated myself to some nice new ones purely for this) in a very rough style. There is no refinement and perfection. It doesn't need it.

You might choose to use a digital document or notebook, or journal it. Find a way that works for you. I like the feel of a physical, tangible object. And, as I say, I bloody love stationery (I actually may have an addiction), so any excuse.

Since I first mentioned this online a few other freelancers in my network have joined me in doing this. It is so nice to see the idea spreading and joy being shared.

If you head to fallingofftheladder.com/blog/little-book-of-epic-wins, you can see some examples of my doodleness and joy.

Social proof folder

This is a folder on my computer which contains official testimonials from clients, as well as screenshots of any lovely comments made via email, social media or online chats – anywhere someone said something about me that was complimentary.

It cannot be understated how powerful these are for helping you to recognise your progress and successes. These are words from other fabulous humans, people that appreciate you and your work, or even just make a lovely comment on one of your social media posts.

It is powerful stuff, especially when you are having a wobble or doubting your existence.

Project book

This is a notebook (yes, more stationery) where I simply record each project I do, who it is for, the rate I charged, how I got the work, the ups and downs of each project, and anything else noteworthy.

This has been a particularly handy reminder when a client comes back six to twelve months later wanting another project – and you have forgotten in the meanwhile the various pain points that you might want to account for now in any new contact, and whether you even want to take it on.

Testimonials

Don't be too shy to ask for testimonials – and to share them. It is not bragging; it is sharing your expertise. It is showing the value you can offer and why you are different to your competitors.

I have only started doing this recently and it is a great little confidence booster. It also has the added bonus of regularly showing you that you are indeed marvellous.

Testimonials will often reflect your personality – your customers know you and will write about you from a position of having worked with you. One of mine states outright that I am a loon. A clever one who knows their stuff, but a loon no less.

> *Testimonials will often reflect your personality. One of mine states outright that I am a loon*

It doesn't have to be when a project is over. If you have repeat work from a client, make sure you ask for one midway through. Get them on your website and ask them to submit it via LinkedIn recommendations as well.

Not only are testimonials great for publicity – potential clients do read them – they can also often give you a good insight into the value you provide, and possibly hadn't even realised. You may find that the value you offer shifts over time, and it could vary depending on the client and project. This is also why it is important to get regular feedback so you can see what are the common appreciated traits that you offer and where your value is the strongest.

For example, one of my clients was really happy with my work because of how patient and flexible I had been on our project. If you had asked me what value I thought I had provided, I'd have made some comment about how I had done some templates and guidelines upfront to help and just done quality work. But the thing that had really stuck in her mind was me switching things around a lot to ease their burden and deadlines, and having dealt with it all in a calm and patient manner, not getting fazed by anything.

This was quite the eye-opener for me – patient and flexible are not words that would have been used to describe me in any of my previous permanent roles working for others. My continual frustrations, tiredness and stress meant that I was highly strung, tense and did not deal well with uncertainty. But this new lifestyle I have created has led to an almost total change in demeanour. I had never even noticed the shift in the value I offer until I received this testimonial – and it really put a smile on my face, thinking how I would never have been described this way just a year before and, in fact, had been told the very opposite.

My year in numbers

At the end of every business and calendar year I create an infographic of 'my year in numbers'. This is a way of condensing some of the figures in my business. It can be anything from the number of clients won that year, how many business books I have read, the hours put into a certain project, to the number of learning modules built. You can record anything you like. They have sparked quite a bit of conversation when I have shared them online too.

You can see some of mine at www.unlikelygenius.com/blog

> "One thing I have learned to do is to value, appreciate and celebrate my successes. That's a good mindset to have, I reckon."
> **Jo**

Indeed it is.

These little records are the best way to see how you change, even transform, to remember the good bits rather than the negatives and tough stuff. You really will forget just how far you have come and all the little things that happen week to week. I have a shocking memory, so I amaze myself when I look back through these.

As an added benefit, they will also give you things to talk about in your social media and promotions. They will help you grow your visibility and help your reputation and how your audience perceives you.

They can also help to prevent you becoming stuck or stagnant. They are essentially tools to use to review your progress against your goals, priorities, direction, interests, skills and projects. All of these will grow with you. You'll be able to recap which skills you have learnt and which you now need to level up.

The transformation is on your own terms, which is even more satisfying. You have worked your butt off, but for yourself. That is to be celebrated.

Just make sure you review your achievements against your own definition of success and how work should look. That's exactly where we'll start.

You know what you need to do! Buy that stationery and get cracking.

Which of the ideas here might you try? Or have you got some ideas of your own?

....
....
....
....
....
....

What examples can you think of from the last week or so to record in a little book of epic wins or an infographic?

....
....
....
....
....
....

I SHOULD HAVE STARTED HERE

> "It's all about the choice. It's MINE. My business and my
> finances are about my vision of success, no one else's."
> **Joelle**

There are certain things that society, the corporate world, our
families, schools, and any other bugger with an opinion has told
us over the years, as we saw in part one of this book. More than
that – they have not just told us, they have **instilled** beliefs. And
one of the first things you need to do when working for yourself
is to look at these beliefs. See which ones serve you and decide
which ones you need to launch out of the window.

I didn't know this when I first went self-employed – and I wish
someone had told me. I wish I had started there. Also, it isn't as
easy as it sounds.

*You will need
to unravel not
just years, but
a lifetime's (!)
worth of
ingrained
beliefs that
are unlikely to
be your own*

Our current accepted work culture,
and its beliefs and expectations, has
been driven deep into our brains for
decades, so the habits formed by this
way of thinking are hard to shake. You
will need to unravel not just years, but
a lifetime's (!) worth of ingrained beliefs
that are unlikely to be your own.

Just let that settle in for a moment...

A lifetime's worth of someone
else's ideals.

This is something that I still find hard to leave behind, three
years after leaving employment (and being overjoyed to about it).

Although I have come such a long way, I still have to remind myself that I don't have to work nine to five if it doesn't work for me.

I can work in my pyjamas if I like (not that I ever do, before 4pm anyway).

I can work according to my values and dictate what they are.

I can turn down work if it doesn't interest me or my gut is telling me not to. (I was in a 'take everything on' phase for a long time.)

I can hide away when I need to – or be visible when I feel strong enough.

I can rock up to my desk 'late' if I've had a bad night's sleep (a huge bonus for this chronic insomniac).

I can try new things. Whenever I want.

I can do all the self-development I want and don't have to justify why.

I can drink wine in meetings (with a certain client anyway – we like a 4pm Friday wine catch-up).

I can swear.

I can be a sarcastic bugger.

I can cry.

I can laugh.

If I am having an unproductive hour, day or even week, I can walk away from my desk for an hour and do something else until I am ready

to crack on. (At time of writing, I decided to bugger off to the garden centre for an hour today to buy poppies because I was procrastinating, and clearly too middle-aged. And I have taken to a 3pm swim a couple of times a week.)

I can be a big Disney-loving, sloth-adoring child without being told to grow up and be sensible. I can be sensible or tired without being told to cheer up. I can tell my truth without fear of rebuke. I can be giddy without being told to calm down. I can chat with whoever I want at whatever time without knowing every minute is being clocked.

I can take holidays without having to book them months in advance (well, kinda. I haven't quite mastered this one yet) and don't have to justify time out for medical appointments. Or be told I am not allowed to go.

And I can do it all without judgement and 'the face' of begrudging approval ... except that I get that look every day from the diva bunnies and the man.

It is a feeling well recognised by freelancers and the self-employed.

> "... you can concentrate without people distracting or interrupting you. You can physically move around without fear of unwanted interaction; no one will accost you while you make a coffee or use the shredding machine, and hijack half an hour of your time. And if you don't feel you can face anyone at all, you don't have to."
> **Tom Albrighton, *The Freelance Introvert*[13]**

It took time for me to realise the wealth of possibilities with working from home and being my own boss, but it is this very realisation that has led to me finally being comfortable in my own skin again. To feel like I can be myself and I should not be embarrassed about it. Or ashamed.

In return I have had such lovely feedback about how enjoyable it is to work with me on projects, how clients have had fun and enjoy our meetings but also feel really productive. My clients love updates (or guest appearances) from my rabbits and that I do all of this while being an 'expert' and really showing what I know. If that doesn't show that you don't have to be a robot, I don't know what would.

Of course, there are some clients that prefer you to be a little more serious than others, but you soon get the gist of what is expected from first communications. Generally, the more visible you get, and the more your business reflects you, the more you see an increase in attracting like-minded individuals and companies. And, actually, some of my most stony-faced clients have finally let their walls down when faced with a rather fluffy face on Zoom. It has changed relationships for the better.

It is also quite reciprocal when you find someone you just don't gel with. I have made the mistake of still accepting these jobs in the past, but I am promising myself I won't do any more. This was, in fact, partly what fuelled my resolution for 2021.

> "In 2021, I will only take on projects which excite me and bring me joy."

One of the biggest things I have had to redefine was my definition of success.

From school and throughout our careers we are told that success means climbing the ladder, becoming management, CEO or head of whatever department. It's continual promotions and heading for the next bigger and better thing. It is managing a team of people, winning awards, or landing or serving big-budget clients. Heading for a bigger wage and the magical six figures.

Some of this still applies in self-employment (each to their own), but it certainly isn't the only marker of success. Depending on your beliefs and goals you might not put much stock in any of that and find it quite superficial.

In many of my chats with fellow freelancers, it has become apparent that we tend to value things like achieving a work-life balance, getting to spend more time with the family, restoring our mental and physical health, working on projects we want to work on, and having a flexible schedule. There is a power that comes with now being in charge of your own journey. On the change self-employment has brought, Kate says, "A weight has lifted from my shoulders. I feel free and ready to make my own challenges."

> "A weight has lifted from my shoulders. I feel free and ready to make my own challenges" – Kate

It feels like the pretentiousness has fallen away and everything is just so much more ... real. Honest. There is a vulnerability that shows, and a humanity.

Another marvellous benefit of working for yourself is that any successes are your own – not your manager's, not belonging to the whole team, the business or conniving team members, who are there to steal the limelight. There is a real feeling of pride in that. You can say, "I did that." Just little old me. And that is also a real confidence builder.

My initial view of success at starting out was to just win some work/contracts to get started, to get the flexibility I needed in my life for medical appointments, and to improve my mental and physical health, and hopefully in the process relieve the pain levels I was battling with daily.

As I have gone along and achieved some of those goals, I have shifted the goalposts.

I have added being 'comfortable' with the wage I am bringing in. (I never had a set number in mind, but just knew it needed to be more than the wage I was on in my last permanent role and the aim now is to just increase it year on year.) I also added to keep learning new things, and to find ways of expanding my offerings and bringing in passive income. I have established my values and these too guide my work (we'll come to these later).

By having defined success, I can increase the steps I take and make sure they are my priority

This year I also added in my goal to have written and published this book – even if only two people buy it, to have written and published a book will be one of my life's goals ticked off and I have chosen to deem that a success (as you're reading it, I'm halfway there). If I get it into a bookshop, that will be the next level!

My final definition of success is to achieve some semblance of life balance. I am terrible for taking on too much and getting too giddy – I'm a people pleaser. I am trying so hard this year to say no to some things and to give myself some time and space to rest and enjoy my hobbies, and do the side projects I want to do. I actually took two months off paid client work (unheard of for me) to complete this book and crack on with Be The Future – an environmental side project of which I am one of the co-founders.

By defining my interpretation of success in this way, I can take incremental steps towards them and make sure they are my priority. I can amend my definition over time, as I grow and as the business develops. This is something that Grace Marshall sums up perfectly in *Struggle*.[14]

> "In truth, my personal definition of success has grown incrementally over the years, with each decision, each project, each client. When something chimes well, I grow a little bolder and shine a little brighter. But when something jars, that sharpens my clarity like nothing else. That's when my understanding grows exponentially."

Now, you get to redefine your life by your own terms.

I am excited for what you might come up with.

OVER TO YOU

What beliefs do you still hold about work and yourself
which were actually instilled by others, the work culture or
your education?

....

....

....

....

Are they actually true? How do you need to redefine
your beliefs?

....

....

....

....

How would you define success now (for you, no one else)?

....

....

....

....

What will success look like for you in your own business?

....

....

....

....

CAN'T I JUST BE WHELMED?

After the euphoria of making the leap, the freedom of self-employment can bring its own brain-frying side effects, such as decision paralysis, people pleasing, a nervous energy and, sometimes, overwhelm. These are all perfectly natural feelings.

It can be very daunting to now have all this power. To be the one who has to make all the decisions. To know the responsibility for everything is firmly in your hands. Especially if you're as rubbish as I am at making decisions – I can't even decide what to have for lunch most days – so it takes extra-strong brain reserves to decide on the important stuff.

To go from being fully controlled to having full control is one hell of a leap. You may feel like you have been thrown in at the deep end. This is where the decision paralysis can hit – when you get so afraid of the many outcomes whirring around your brain (and fixating on the bad ones) that you freeze. You hope the decision will make itself or you attempt to avoid making it altogether.

> "I was in analysis paralysis because I second-guessed myself at every turn, and the consequences of making the wrong decision seemed catastrophic."
> **Denise Duffield-Thomas, *Chillpreneur*[15]**

Many self-employed people work alone at home and so may not have someone else's brains to pick or the opportunity to easily get a second opinion, so it can feel quite stressful and lonely if you get stuck in a loop. But this is where your online connections come in, and there is always someone looking for a few minutes' procrastination who will be willing to give an opinion.

A lot of overwhelm comes down to doubting ourselves and our abilities. There is also an element in finding the right balance of control and responsibility. Although you are working for yourself, you don't HAVE to do everything yourself. Sometimes it is smarter to get help, to let go of a little control. It can actually ease stress and loneliness.

Control can be hard to let go of when the business is your own. It's hard to delegate and hand over responsibility of any tasks to others. You might feel the need to keep a tight leash on everything, and make sure it is up to your standards and that it all gets done at the right time in the right way. I certainly felt that way at first.

BUT...

It is important to remind yourself that this is likely to be a significant reason why you went solo – to have autonomy and be able to make decisions for yourself, to focus on the work you enjoy. And it is a skill you can practise and get more comfortable with doing. You may well find that once you hand over the bits you don't like doing to someone else, and it goes well, that you suddenly want to give loads away and really hone the tasks you do. (Not speaking from experience at all here ... hmm.)

Sometimes it is smarter to get help, to let go of a little control. It can actually ease stress and loneliness

Remember:

- You chose self-employment to have more control over your life and work – so embrace it. Have fun with it.
- Control means that you get to be able to work according to your values and work towards those other perks you are hoping for (more family time, flexibility, whatever it is for you).
- You don't have to take everything on your shoulders. Ask for help. Hire help. Ask opinions. Bend someone's ear.
- All the experience you bring to the business. Just because you are new to self-employment, doesn't mean you are new to work. You have knowledge and skills!

Get to know the signs of your overwhelm. I can say, from experience, there will always be some days which catch you off guard and swoop you off into their current, but the better you get at recognising your warning signs, the more proactive you can be in preventing the burnout to which these little rabbit holes can lead. I have come to recognise that I am overwhelmed and overworked when, more often than not, the smallest thing becomes a big deal and tips me over a precipice – it's usually a comment or complication that I know I could have handled better on another day but today it resulted in stress, tears or hiding away.

When I lose my motivation and creativity, it is a sign to me that I have gone too far away from my values and goals (and should've already spotted it sooner). I am usually ridiculously engaged and motivated, so as soon as I utter the words 'I can't be arsed', I know I have a problem.

OVER TO YOU

What are the signs that you are starting to feel
overwhelmed?

....
....
....
....
....

What actions could you put in place to help you rectify it
sooner, before the overwhelm strikes?

....
....
....
....
....

WHEN I'M BIG I WANT TO BE … SMALL

An aspect of running a business that I have had to consider a lot is growth and what that looks like for me. Again, it is an area that is preconceived by work culture and industry, and takes some redefining.

As soon as you become more visible and clients start flooding in, the questions begin.

"Are you going to hire a team?"

"Do you want to become an agency?"

"How are you going to grow/scale?"

"What is your five-year business plan?"

"Are you going to take on an office space?"

Or the more presumptuous "When are you going to hire staff?"

Eurgh.

What these people (usually fully initiated and ingrained in the corporate world) fail to realise is that these presumptions are no longer in line with your definition of success. Growth does not have to be about hiring staff, changing your title to be CEO, Director or some made-up nonsense. Or winning the biggest-named clients. You might not need a premises outside the home for your mountains of stock. It doesn't have to be about hiring a team.

That is no longer in line with my definition of success and growth. I didn't go into self-employment to start hiring others and building an empire. I am guessing it is not the case for many of you too.

I chose self-employment for the flexibility I needed in my life, to find balance with my physical and mental health, and to find a way to enjoy working. We spend a lot of our hours working and it is important to enjoy it, or at least not to be driven to daily panic attacks because of it. Luckily, I found all this and a whole lot more.

If it is not right for you, trust your gut and push back. Explain how you define growth now, and what is important to you

Francesca's reasons for going solo were far from being about growth in a 'traditional' sense. Employment and the office space were making it very difficult to manage the eating disorder that was putting her life at risk.

"With all the diet and food talk that inevitably goes on in office environments – even just the mundane 'What are you having for tea?' – to the endless birthday cakes, rewards in the form of food and drink such as team lunches or after work drinks, and stinky fish cooked in the office microwave, it makes a challenging environment for anyone with difficulties around food. Diet talk is the worst. Why is that a way for people to bond?"

The growth she needed was one of recovery and having the space to regain her health. She needed to find a way of working which gave her the flexibility to focus on herself and help her recovery.

There are a myriad of personal challenges which are hindered by the traditional office space, yet this doesn't even tend to appear in conversation, and certainly few adaptations are made. Requests go unanswered. I even asked to be moved from near the kitchen in one role due to my sensitivity to sounds and smells, only to be moved right next to the door a couple of months later. It is that lack of understanding, or lack of attempt to understand, that brings gaslighting to mind.

Sometimes, the reason for going solo is purely to escape these environments. There is not even a flicker of wanting to grow or build a team. Though I have started using subcontractors occasionally where needed, I am not looking to start hiring staff, or becoming an agency. This kind of growth adds a layer of complication and management that I am so glad is out of my life. It also takes me away from doing the work I enjoy – the actual creative stuff. Why would I want to give that to anyone else?

You may want to build an empire, and that is fabulous. The even more fabulous thing is, you don't have to decide any of this right now. You can just get cracking and see how things evolve. The key is not to let others infiltrate your brain. To pressure you into scaling. As you network or hire a coach, these things can be suggested, perhaps even pushed on you, quite heavily. If it is not right for you, trust your gut and push back. Explain how you define growth now, and what is important to you.

If you do want to make some decisions so that you have something to aim for and you just can't quite yet tear yourself away from plans and proposals, then you definitely need to think about what you want. Not what your family, society or even recruitment people tell you. What is best for you? What brings you joy in your work? Where are you happiest and what aspects of work do you most enjoy?

Start from there and, most importantly, be open and reflect often. You never know what may be around the corner or where you may take yourself.

OVER TO YOU

Make some notes below on how you would define growth for you and the business, considering:

- Your reasons for going solo

....
....
....

- Your mindset and emotions

....
....
....

- Your confidence

....
....
....

- Whether you want to manage others rather than doing the actual client work

....
....
....

- The skills you want to develop

....
....
....

- The tasks that you enjoy most

....
....
....

WOBBLY BITS

> "It's okay to feel all of the stuff you're feeling. You're just becoming human again. You're not doing life wrong; you're doing it right. If there's any secret you're missing, it's that doing it right is just really hard."
> **Glennon Doyle, *Untamed*[16]**

Let's not sugar-coat it – you will have wobbles along the way.

I am not talking about my ample, wobbly, work-from-home bottom here. I mean those moments of tears, low mood, doubts you can do this, and hiding under your desk. Or perusing the job search websites with thoughts of maybe I should just have a look at what jobs are out there and consider going back to a permanent role.

There may be crippling moments of doubt. You may be slapped around the face by a bout of imposter syndrome, or comparisonitis may creep up and make you believe you are not hustling like the badass entrepreneur you are supposed to be. You might get bad feedback, lose out on a project, lose a client. You may wind up comparing yourself to other freelancers, some of whom have been doing this a lot longer than you, and/or are in different industries.

You may be slapped around the face by a bout of imposter syndrome

A flipping worldwide pandemic might even hit. In terms of wobbles, that one is off the Richter scale.

It is normal to have a wobble after something momentous has happened – something as momentous as deciding to start a business for sure – but the more prepared you can be for these moments in advance, the better.

> "The wobble that comes after the intensity. It helps to know it's normal, and instead of beating ourselves up with how we think we 'should' feel, to give ourselves space to recover and let the rest of us catch up with what just happened."
> **Grace Marshall,** *Struggle*[17]

That's not to say you will always have an impending sense of doom, but simple tricks such as ensuring your expectations are realistic and catching your self-talk can help.

Expectations is a key word here. If you go into self-employment expecting every day to be sunshine and rainbows, you will be disappointed. No business, no matter how successful, will have a hundred per cent good days. Not even the Nikes and Apples of this world (although I am sure their billions help cushion the blows).

In these wobbly moments you need a plan in place so you can step back and collect yourself and your scattered thoughts. Make sure you are realistic in your expectations about what you can achieve. Make sure that you have aligned your expectations with your reframed definition of success and what work is to you.

Could you:

- Give yourself time out to process everything?
- Chat to other self-employed folk who you know have a similar mindset to you?
- Hash out your thoughts in a journal – maybe with some ready-made prompts to help order your thinking?
- Look back at your little book of epic wins and social proof folder?
- Ask a current client for some feedback and what they think is working well so far?
- Ask a friend, spouse or family member for something positive or something you are good at?

- Take time out and do something you enjoy? This is as important as getting shit done. (I am such a hypocrite as this is always the first thing to slide for me.)

These may seem like fairly small things, but sometimes having just an ounce of validation can be enough to at least help you plough on for another day and to shut that browser window with a job board on it or block a call from a recruiter.

However, if you are anything like me and actually get upset, more often than not when someone says something nice to you – prepare to whisper a thank you for their kind words and move on before the flood gates open.

The other source of the wobbles is when something goes wrong. Big or small (and easier said than done), don't beat yourself up too much. Especially for the small.

I'm pretty sure we all have moments where we undercharge, under/overestimate the length of time it will take to do something, forget to plan in the 7,000 rounds of amends a customer wants, post something on social media and instantly regret it, take on that project we had a bad feeling about and get bitten on the arse as a result, are short with a rude client who is doing our head in, or one of a gazillion other things we can easily berate ourselves over.

In fact, a quick glimpse at any of the freelance groups I am in tells me this is so, with daily cries of "How would you deal with...?", "I think I've messed up. HELP!", "What would you do...?" or "Is this client taking advantage?"

When you are doing everything yourself and juggling multiple clients, as you often are when running a business, it is easy to drop the ball. By reframing these moments as a learning curve,

133

noting the experience down somewhere you can look back at it, and doing whatever you can to improve the situation now, you will become stronger for it. Maybe even put some new processes in place to prevent it happening again.

Over time, if you can manage your expectations and responses, you may even start to be able to shrug some things off with a 'oh well, it's part of running a business', then crack on and deal with it, rather than tying yourself in knots with worry. The things that bother you today will not be the same things that bother you in six months' time.

It may even make you a better decision-maker, as Pavitra found. "Self-employment has improved my decision-making ability. Accepting a project as a freelancer means taking all aspects such as deadlines, subject-matter expertise and the relationship with the client into consideration. Not to mention, most decisions have to be taken under a time crunch; you really need to have an efficient thought process in place to accept or reject potential projects."

There will also be times that you have to do things you don't enjoy or aren't necessarily good at and these can make the self-doubt crawl back into your ear, whispering its sweet nothings and encouraging you along the path to Wobble Town.

In Elizabeth Gilbert's *Big Magic*, Mark Manson asks, "What's your favourite flavour of shit sandwich?" The idea behind posing this question is to consider that "Everything sucks, some of the time."[18] He is asking what is your favourite shitty thing to do? And goes on to establish the expectations that nothing is all unicorns and bouncing bunnies.

I love this reframe – yes, there are some things we hate doing, but running your own business is on the whole a marvellous affair, so those crappy tasks you dislike are at least your favourite type of shit sandwich filler, wedged between the spongy goodness of tasty sourdough bread. Mmm mmmm.

For me, the shit sandwich filler is quoting, pitching, accounting, and managing my website. But the beautiful bread (oh, how I love bread) is the fact that I can outsource this stuff and just get on with doing what I do best – the creative work and dealing with the clients.

The things that bother you today will not be the same things that bother you in six months' time

There will always be a task you don't like amidst the stuff you love doing.

Every fabulous team has that one person that grates on someone.

Every amazing day where you feel at the top of the world can still contain a snarky email or a troublesome online troll.

You may present an idea that seems amazing to you but gets rejected outright by the client. We all know the story of J.K. Rowling getting rejected with *Harry Potter* a gazillion times, right? (I really didn't get on with it but millions, and my nephew, disagree.)

It is how you deal with these 'side effects' that makes the difference. How you ensure that they don't bring you down or throw you off course. Some days, no matter how hard you try, they will get to you. They may ruin your mood. How you pick yourself up is the important question.

After a few cock-ups of my own creation I have just got to that point (most of the time anyway) and I have learnt the few tools that will help me (yoga, breathing exercises, mindfulness, cuddling bunnies, swimming, screaming into the abyss). And there are certainly days where something unexpected totally throws me and nothing other than starting fresh the next day can help. In some cases, I will never learn.

If all else fails, take a leaf out of Kate's book and just think back to that moment of escape: "Handing my notice in is one of the greatest things I've ever done for myself and my self-worth. I still feel rejuvenated by that feeling whenever I have a wobble."

OVER TO YOU

Have a wobble plan – who can you call when you have a crisis? What is the most effective method for calming your wobbles?

....
....
....
....
....
....

It is worth tracking what sets off any wobbles so you can put some pre-emptive measures in place for next time.

....
....
....
....
....
....

When mid-wobble, what is your main worry? Is it valid? How can you get past it? Who can help? What do you need to stabilise your mind?

....
....
....
....
....
....

TAKING THE GOOD WITH THE BAD

As mentioned previously, I am unbelievably BAD at taking praise. I have that true British awkwardness that emerges with my blushes as soon as anyone says anything nice. I fluster and pass the praise onto someone else. I don't know where to look. I turn a dazzling shade of beetroot, mumble a thanks and try desperately to provide an 'excuse' for doing well. I may even burst into happy but embarrassed tears. I have no idea why I respond this way, but it is like some rabid monkeys have taken over my brain and are holding it hostage until the danger has gone away. Luckily, I am slightly better at taking criticism (if it's constructive).

Taking feedback and commentary on your work (and the way you run your business) is something you have to learn to cope with when self-employed – whether you call it amends, points for development or feedback, it will be coming to you, and it will feel personal. There is no buffer as it passes through a hierarchy. While the wins are all yours, so are the problems, criticisms, off-piste ideas and general cock-ups.

When I recently raised my issues with taking praise, a fellow freelancer quite rightly responded, "All you need to do is say thank you, and move on." Hardly groundbreaking, yet to me it kinda was. I have wholeheartedly adopted this technique for any feedback.

The power in maintaining a positive mindset throughout this process is in how you reframe feedback. Don't call it 'criticism', 'stuff I did wrong', or let imposter syndrome start wittering in your ear – as corny as it sounds, think of it as points for development.

Pavitra explains that learning how to handle criticism objectively was a big mindset shift for her and she had to reframe it in this way. "In my initial years as a freelance translator, negative comments by reviewers would throw me into depths of despair. Days on end, I would wallow around in self-pity. It took me quite some time to develop a thick skin to analyse the reviewers' comments. I realised that negative comments actually help you assess your work objectively. In hindsight, I am a better translator, thanks to my reviewers. Because of them, I can identify my weak areas and work on improving them."

Negative comments actually help you assess your work objectively

This is what is most commonly referred to as a growth mindset,[19] where you learn from criticism, embrace challenges, and find lessons and inspiration through a desire to learn. Those with a fixed mindset, on the other hand, struggle to take criticism on board, feel threatened by the success of others and give up easily.

The interesting thing I have found is that a lot of my current clients feel even more awkward than I do during feedback. They will apologise endlessly for asking for amends, or for a tweak to be made to a design. When you have built a relaxed relationship with people, as I like to, it is great for the overall project but can sometimes feel like you are giving or taking feedback from a friend. Awkward. Though if they are apologising for the inconvenience of having amends, I will also reassure them that it is absolutely fine, and that is what this process is for (so long as this isn't round 37 of sending over two amends at a time).

I often find that there are patterns in the feedback and they help me to identify where I might need to change part of my process, or make sure I more thoroughly check part of a project before it goes out. It identifies the places that I don't give enough attention to, or rush. And tasks where I would have benefitted from stepping back before coming back to it. Occasionally, I will even learn a new way of doing something through responding to amends.

Sometimes I may not agree with the requested amends, but if there is a justifiable reason for the change, I just crack on and do it. If it is totally illogical, I will explain to the client why and propose an alternative solution. A joy of working at home alone is being able to throw a comment or two along the lines of "Seriously? Why the hell would you even want that?" (obvs with more swears and frustration than that gives off) at the computer and get it off your chest.

In short - process the comment(s), rectify (if needed), feed back on the feedback, and move on.

OVER TO YOU

How do you deal with criticism? Think back to times you have received it and how it felt.

....
....
....
....
....
....

How could you reframe it to make it feel better?

....
....
....
....
....
....

What can you put in place to learn from it? For example, are there any new processes you could put in place to avoid the issue occurring in future work?

....
....
....
....
....
....

SURVIVAL INSTINCT

> "You don't know your own strength until you're forced to dig yourself out of the deepest holes of your own mind."
> **Joelle**

Three years ago, my fears were around not progressing as I 'should', of the next time I'd be dragged into HR to be questioned about my absence record, of the next panic attack taking hold and having to hide in the toilets. Of not being given the 'good' projects to work on or being overlooked for yet another opportunity. Of continually being scared that I had said or done something wrong again.

It started to breed paranoia too – though some of my fears turned out to be perfectly valid concerns. When this fear is not dealt with, it creates a permanent state of anxiety and, potentially, depression.

These days, I am so relieved to have moved away from that state and though I still have fears, they are now around very different things, and certainly not as all-consuming. Mostly, they revolve around getting bad feedback, unpaid invoices and my imposter syndrome telling me that one day soon I will be found out. Found out for what? I have no idea. But I feel it. That is the whole point of imposter syndrome.

When you are someone that wants to do their best at all times, is ambitious and is learning to do new things, there will always be a level of fear. We all need a certain level of fear to survive, though you'd all be okay if a grizzly bear came along as I'd either:

a) Cuddle it, and be eaten.
b) Attempt to run away, fall flat on my face, and be eaten.

Bizarrely, for someone with anxiety, I have never been the biggest fan of letting fear control me and stopping me doing the things I want to do in my personal life – which is why I have a history of flinging myself off things, into things and maybe being a bit riskier than my parents would have liked. It is why I have done a bungee jump, dived with sharks, and undertaken gruelling challenges for charity. It's why I want to do a skydive (I think).

When you are someone that wants to do their best at all times, is ambitious and is learning to do new things, there will always be a level of fear

But fear around your work life just feels that bit more raw and real. The 'what's the worst that could happen?' feels more likely to happen and life-changing. It's personal, in a different way. It's public. It can create shame and embarrassment if it goes wrong.

Once you acknowledge the fear and work out what it is holding you back from it, only then can you move towards it. Or throw yourself at it (or trip into it in my case).

Fear of bad reviews really got to me in the process of planning this book, but I have (with the help of Elizabeth Gilbert and Denise Duffield-Thomas) realised that reviews are not mine to control and are a necessary evil. If you want to put your creativity and work out in the world, and achieve your goals, you must take the wildly differing opinions that come with it. Attracting polarising views means you have created something that has flared up passioned responses. It's much better than being average or ignored. (Please remind me of this later.)

> "If you dare to create something and put it out there, after all, then it may accidentally stir up a response... If people enjoy what you have created, terrific. If people ignore what you've created, too bad. If people misunderstand why you have created – don't sweat it. And what if people absolutely hate what you have created? What if people attack you with savage vitriol, and insult your intelligence, and malign your motives, and drag your good name through the mud?
>
> Just smile sweetly and suggest – as politely as you possibly can – that they go make their own fucking art.
>
> Then stubbornly continue making yours."
> **Elizabeth Gilbert, *Big Magic*[20]**

I also realised that I have given other wildly successful household-name authors one- or two-star reviews, so why wouldn't a mere mortal like me receive them at some point? I still fear the nasty reviews somewhat – there is no need for the brutal bile some people put forth – but I am no longer letting it hold me back (gets on my knees and pleads for a lovely review from you, kind reader person, thank you, please).

I found a way to step towards my goal. I knew I wanted to write but never thought I could or should. I don't use enough big, flouncy words. I couldn't tell you what half the grammar terms mean (a Year 4 child had to teach me what a subjunctive clause was back when I was a teaching assistant). I write in a very conversational manner.

But I found ways to build my confidence and confront the fear in steps.

I started by writing a blog post once a week for 52 weeks with a fabulous group called #Write52 over on Twitter. We all made the same commitment, to write every week for a year on the theme of our choosing. We 'just' had to commit to doing it. And I did!

I'm in the Write52 Hall of Fame and everything.[21] The progress I made in my wiring and confidence rocketed during this time. I even guest edited the weekly email newsletter one week, a huge leap in itself for me.

Next, I started to write for an industry journal. The response to those articles has provided encouragement that I can write and I do have something useful to say. I even won the award for article of the year and am now getting requests to do more writing for them, such as book reviews. Writing for different topics and purposes in this way is a great way to practice.

Finally, I have surrounded myself with writers and I am absorbing the knowledge of others, reading around the craft of writing, and watching what others do.

Love it or hate it, there does appear to be something in this pushing out of your comfort zone. By pushing myself through my fears, I have had opportunities come my way that I wouldn't have had otherwise.

I found ways to build my confidence and confront the fear in steps

Back in February 2020, I declared, "I will never do video!" Not a chance. No way. A couple of months later, after being gently prodded by a fellow business owner, I was enrolled in the Videotastic course (see the resources section) about finding your confidence on camera and using video in your business.

I really didn't think I would actually do it. I appeared to have some logic that I would give our mentor, Becky Holmes, a challenge. I figured I had nothing to lose. But within a few weeks I had started creating a course of my own to sell on my website, which uses a lot of video. I was getting increasingly comfortable on camera. I also started getting video interviews requested for all kinds of capers, and I was getting repeated requests from potential clients who had seen my mush out there. I even started to appear on podcasts – something that a year before would have been unfathomable to me, on account of me hating the sound of my voice on recordings and being so fearful of making a fool of myself. The course pushed me to make baby steps and provided a safe, supportive environment to practise with no judgement. And it opened a world of opportunities.

Acknowledge the fear and let it fire you on

Even when stubbornly entrenched in your comfort zone, with your PJs on and a glass of wine in hand, there are ways to take advantage of little avenues that open up to see if something new can work for you. You don't have to take huge leaps of faith. Something new could be you stubbornly thinking you will give someone a challenge, or wanting to test the waters in a new area.

Acknowledge the fear and let it fire you on.

If you ever want to see the ultimate 'fuck it moment', check out *The Greatest Showman* "This Is Me" with Keala Settle on YouTube.[22] God love her. 72.7 million views and counting ... they can't all be mine.

OVER TO YOU

What fears are holding you back?

....

....

....

....

....

What would you like to do but are fearful of the outcome?
What are the potential outcomes – good and bad?

....

....

....

....

....

List your thoughts, and take action to do one of them
today. It could be sign up to a course, email someone
you would really love to work with, book in a photoshoot,
contact someone about appearing on their podcast. Note
how you feel about it. Why is the fear there?

....

....

....

....

....

Once you have done your thing, note how you feel. Is it relief? Excitement? Nervous trepidation?

....

....

....

....

....

....

PRIORITISING YOUR WHY

Priorities means different things to different people, and it isn't always easy to see how or where to start with establishing them. Here, we are considering your personal priorities – for you, your life and that of your family (nothing to do with priorities relating to scheduling work).

As a corporate escapee, your priorities are likely to be closely linked to why you have made (or want to make) the leap into self-employment. For example, is it for more time with your family? Your health? To relocate? To earn more money? To save your sanity?

Sometimes, you just might realise that you are working your butt off for others, when, actually, you could be reaping the rewards yourself

For me, there were many reasons, but the most urgent was to help my health, which was declining by the day, with each health issue exacerbating the next under the intense stress my body was under. Add in chronic insomnia and acute pain, and my resilience for the whole environment was dropping daily. It was also clear I had no route of progression, I would never fit, and I needed flexibility in my days for insomnia and medical appointments.

When the opportunity for self-employment presented itself, I realised that this could actually give me what I needed. I had nothing to lose and that those things I desperately wanted and needed were really possible.

Sometimes, you just might realise that you are working your butt off for others, when, actually, you could be reaping the rewards yourself. Sophie says, "I think if you're one of the most proactive people in your workplace, then you should probably be doing it for yourself, not somebody else."

It is a sentiment that Jo also echoes. "I actually loved the job I was in at the time of the leap, but I realised that the love of which I speak had meant I'd given so much extra of myself to that role and not dedicated enough of my time and energy to building agoodwriteup as much as I could have done. That love also meant that I never kicked up a fuss each year when there was 'no money' for a raise (even in line with inflation), or when my boss (the business owner) would turn up with a lovely new car or jet off for a fab city break somewhere every time that there was a success in the business that I'd led on. I just felt that if I could give so much and achieve so much for someone else's business, then imagine what would happen with my own!"

Outsourcing is a life raft among the choppy seas

Then there is Francesca, who has an incredibly powerful priority for her business – saving her life. "I nearly died of anorexia. Many times. I was about to die and I started freelancing as something to do from Mum and Dad's sofa. Freelancing is on my terms. Meals in the diary, no working after hours unless I choose to, plus the ability to work from home – I really struggle to eat in front of people, so it's a massive difference."

Your reasons for leaping are a great starting place for assessing your priorities. The next step is to think a bit more broadly. Don't just focus on that one leap-inducing reason, particularly if that is likely to become a thing of the past once you have left that employment, such as a certain person causing you hell or being unable to drop to part-time hours. You now need to think with a forward focus.

Looking into your crystal ball, what are the priorities for:

- You?
- Your new business?
- Your family?
- Your health?
- Anything else?

And, crucially, look with open eyes at where any of these might be in conflict with one another. You may be leaving a career as you want to spend more time with your family, but starting a new business is not a small feat, and may, in fact, take you away from your family more until you get going. Is this something you are prepared to do?

There are many responsibilities that come with running a business to add into your already busy life and there will be times that you need to delegate or prioritise, so you need to be clear from the outset what your priorities are.

When it comes to those tasks you don't enjoy doing, this is where outsourcing is a life raft among the choppy seas. This may feel like a big commitment, to be paying out money for these things at the start of your business, but keep in mind that it may take you hours to do that unenjoyable task that likely results in you wanting to launch your computer out of the window. If you gave it to a specialist in that area or a virtual assistant (VA), they could do it in less time than you'd spend Googling the damn thing, with the bonus that it would help to reduce your stress levels, give you more headspace to focus where needed and free up your time to be doing the things you enjoy.

I am terrible with numbers and find it an absolute chore to do the most basic of sums. I just don't understand anything to do with tax, VAT and the like; therefore, having an accountant was a non-negotiable for me. This has also undoubtedly saved me from a load of stress and from being fined oodles of money by HMRC too as I would have definitely have gotten myself in trouble if I had even attempted it myself.

I also realised I was not the biggest fan of scheduling social media posts and it would take me hours of faffing, struggling to make a decision and frustration. So, I offloaded that job to my ridiculously efficient VA, who gets a month's worth of Twitter scheduled for me in under an hour. I can be carrying on with client work while she ticks away in the background. AND it also means it gets done rather than being repeatedly put back (or not completed) as I knock it further and further down my list of priorities, which was the case 99 per cent of the time.

Once you have your priorities, you can start to think about where your boundaries lie and how these can feed into your values (both coming up).

OVER TO YOU

Write down your priorities for:

- You

....

....

....

....

- Your new business

....

....

....

....

- Your family

....

....

....

....

- Your health

....

....

....

....

- Other

....

....

....

....

Which of these are most important? Your priority priority,
if you will.

....
....
....
....

Which are non-negotiable?

....
....
....
....

Can you see any possible conflicts appear with any?

....
....
....
....
....
....

WHEN THE LINE IS CROSSED

Boundaries, boundaries, wherefore art thou?

Christ if I know.

This is a word that has come up time and time again for me these last few years. Usually as a chant from coaches and fellow freelancers who have repeatedly spotted that this is an area where I let myself down. So, what are they?

Brené Brown explains, "Boundaries are simply: what's okay, and what's not okay."[23] Sounds easy, right? Hmmmm.

The good news is that she goes on to say, "We are not comfortable setting boundaries. Because we care more about what people will think, we don't want to disappoint anyone, we want everyone to like us. And boundaries are not easy."

Maintaining boundaries is definitely an area where my people pleasing tendencies get the better of me. I try to second-guess how a client feels and how much money they have and so knock my own prices down before they have even had a chance to say anything about them. I struggle to raise the topic of an annual rate rise. I take on too much work because I don't want to let anyone down. I have done free work and taken free "Can I pick your brain?" calls. I have let people request last-minute 'urgent' (it never is) work, which has meant I have had to work stupid hours or all weekend to get it done, and not charged a premium for this.

These are common occurrences with people starting out and with those lacking assertiveness or the confidence to push back.

Safe to say, I am far from the expert with boundaries. The thing is I can see how important it is to have boundaries and I can help others work this out, but when it comes to my own, I bash through the mother truckers with reckless abandon.

But I am getting better – just gaining the awareness I was rubbish at it was quite the step forward, and I have started to push back a lot more over the last year. However, I still have a country mile or 10 to go. But as usual, it is something that gets demoted to the bottom of the to-do list. This may be an area we need to work on together, and you can learn from the mistakes I have already made.

> "Those of us who need to get better at holding boundaries rarely have this at the top of our to-do lists. As someone who's generally easy-going and accommodating, it's not until a line gets crossed that I realise where that line is."
> **Grace Marshall, *Struggle*[24]**

What types of boundaries should we be setting?

You will find that you need to establish more boundaries with some clients than others and as you work with more people, you will certainly find new areas to establish boundaries. Some basics to get right from the start are:

- Times when you are available for clients – not just the actual work but responding to emails, phone calls, and so on.
- How those clients are able to contact you – do you have a separate business mobile or are you giving out your personal one? Is it okay if they contact you on WhatsApp at 10pm on a Saturday night? Or 6am on a Monday morning?
- What is included in the project fee and are you getting signed contracts so anything out of scope can be charged for?
- What behaviours will you tolerate? And how will you deal with it? Because, yes, it is possible you may one day get an absolute turnip that is rude to you, maybe even sexist, racist, homophobic or other types of moronic behaviour.

- What are your working hours? Are you going to strictly adhere to them or will you take rush jobs on that may mean you need to work late?
- How are you going to fit in time for self-care and exercise?
- What are your rates? Will you accept negotiation? How much?
- How will you make sure you don't say yes to things you don't want to do?

What happens if these boundaries are broken – at what point would you cease to work with a client?

Once you have defined your boundaries, you need to establish them – to build them into your daily work and processes. Wallpaper your wall with them. Reflect on them regularly. Where relevant, make them clear to your customers – on your website, in your contract, your emails. I have even seen some freelancers have auto-responses to emails, which let clients know that they have set days or times for checking emails so they do not become a constant distraction and affect the flow of work. What a great way to establish a boundary, but also make clear to the client the benefit to them of not being at their beck and call.

Once you have these established, you also need to be clear on what happens if these boundaries are broken – at what point would you cease to work with a client? Are you comfortable to make your feelings known and reaffirm yourself? Have you ensured that you have a get-out clause in your contracts?

As a way to deal with boundary issues, Brené recommends that you remember other people are just doing the best they can. For the first 35 years of her life she says, "I assumed people were sucking on purpose just to piss me off." (Oops, guilty.) But when you assume people are doing the best they can, it makes you a happier person and makes your life better. "The life you change first is your own."[25]

And what about your own personal and home boundaries – such as how you can make yourself down tools at the end of the day? How will you keep your work and personal life separate? How will you make sure you keep up the non-negotiables like family time, sleep and self-care? Will you create a separate workspace in the home where you can close the door on work and switch off?

These are the hardest kinds of boundaries for me, especially when I get giddy about a new project. And I like to tick things off, so will just keep going until things are done, even if it means working late or taking my laptop downstairs. This becomes a habit that is hard to pull back from.

It is not so easy when you are working at home full time. The lines become blurry and it is easy for work to encroach more and more on your downtime. It takes discipline to be able to switch off, and to maintain boundaries. It takes assertion to say "I am not available at weekends" when a customer tramples over the line. If you are responding to customers' emails out of hours, then they will presume it is okay to do the same, and that is a slippery slope. One which I continually slide down on my butt.

Be pro-active in deciding on your boundaries, not reactive

If you are continually breaking the boundaries yourself, well, it's not quite so easy to fire yourself ... but you will certainly need to give yourself a talking to and identify ways to help you get back on track. That might even mean enlisting the force of another person such as a partner or business coach, who can hold you accountable.

How to establish boundaries

Be pro-active in deciding on your boundaries, not reactive. Of course, you can tweak and add to them as you go along, but don't make it up as you go along, as I have. This doesn't treat them with the sincerity and respect they deserve. Being reactive allows a boundary to be trampled and having to deal with a shitty situation before establishing it for future projects, rather than preventing it happening in the first place.

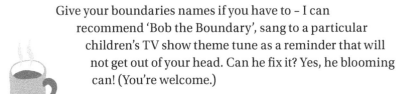

Give your boundaries names if you have to – I can recommend 'Bob the Boundary', sang to a particular children's TV show theme tune as a reminder that will not get out of your head. Can he fix it? Yes, he blooming can! (You're welcome.)

The other way is to devise practices that help to remind you of your boundaries often and to reflect on them.

One way I regularly reflect on boundaries is the project notebook I have on my desk. The way I record projects in this means I have a way of looking at where I can establish boundaries more effectively, among other things. For example, I can easily look back and see that in project B, XYZ was a nightmare. In future, to protect against this, I need to do ABC.

For example, when I look back at one client I have worked for, I am reminded that I found them very difficult to work with as I didn't understand their processes and they didn't fit with my work style. Everything was so illogical and outdated compared to processes I had seen in other companies. Combined with endlessly moving deadlines and goal posts, I started feeling stressed and unhappy with the work. I wasn't giving it my best and the client was quite negative about the work produced at one point as it wasn't to their 'expected style'. So, for the first time ever, I handed my notice in on the contract. While I felt awful doing so, that feeling was soon overtaken with relief and feeling much less stressed and fed up.

As a result, I know in future to a) ensure I get more information up front on processes and get them to explain things better and ask more questions; b) refuse to start the work until I have all the information; or c) if the misalignment with my work style was so vast, not to work for them.

Sometimes it can feel like you are preparing yourself for battle. But hopefully, by planning, there will be less casualties along the way, and you will certainly not be one of them.

A lot of the reluctance to set boundaries, on my part anyway, is the lack of confidence around being assertive, particularly when you first start out and that nagging doubt in your mind says you shouldn't turn work down. Particularly in the early years of self-employment, there is a lot of second-guessing what you are doing, and fear that if you push

Setting boundaries and expectations will help you to move towards your goals and protect yourself and your business

back, the client will go elsewhere or you will have to deal with a confrontation. In reality, when I have pushed back, I have rarely had a bad response. The only people to respond badly have generally been those who were trying to take advantage anyway, and so are not a client I want to work with. You know the type – those plonkers who repeatedly want to knock your prices down, have it 'done yesterday' and that are inevitably late payers – or worse, disappearing acts.

A lot of this I have learnt the hard way. Through a couple of unpaid invoices, or clients that have ghosted me as soon as I have done the concepts for them, and from doing frequent very low-paid jobs when I was freelancing on the side pre-leap. Over time I have got better at spotting the signs, am learning to pay attention to red flags, and being more forthright in my rates.

Setting boundaries and expectations will help you to move towards your goals and protect yourself and your business. But you will need to trust your instincts and be stubborn. Don't let anybody bash those boundaries down.

"Nothing is sustainable without boundaries."
Brené Brown[26]

What boundaries are you setting for yourself and your business?

....

....

....

....

....

Do you accept negotiation on these – from yourself or others? Under what circumstances are you willing to negotiate?

....

....

....

....

....

How do these align with the priorities you identified? Are you protecting those?

....

....

....

....

....

THE MISSING PIECE

One of the hardest things to do after leaving the corporate world can be changing your perception of yourself. I was emotionally battered and bruised, my confidence long since out of the door, so my priority was always to rebuild this.

I felt like every ounce of confidence had all been battered out of me over the last few years, and it resulted in me questioning everything I did, then questioning my questioning, and generally not trusting anyone. I had well and truly lost my identity, and any belief in myself along with it. Something had to change.

And it's not just me. This seems to be a popular truth that is frequently emerging from conversations with other freelancers as to why they have flown the 'safety' of the corporate nest.

Many freelancers and contractors choose to work for themselves in a bid to escape the workplace politics, lack of progression and evils of working under management regimes. While going solo is not a magical fix for all these things, it does help to regain some control and time to be able to rebuild.

Just one year into her self-employment journey Kate says that though there are times when she is very guarded and often consumed with paranoia that her best is simply not good enough, this is balanced out by the benefits – namely having a workday she can control and having the time and space to improve her self-confidence. She makes a very telling statement about her new self-employed life: "I no longer feel I don't deserve good things."

I love that so much. Oh, how I agree too.

Probably 95 per cent of the freelancers I engage with (yes, a totally made-up statistic) regularly state they get imposter syndrome, sometimes cripplingly so. There is a lot of self-doubt and anxiety in the average freelancer's bones, sometimes because of prior experiences, sometimes because of mental health, sometimes because they have just always lacked self-confidence. Maybe it's all of the above; these factors are not mutually exclusive.

However.

Working for ourselves helps us to rebuild our waning confidence.

Bizarrely, leaving the comfort of a full-time permanent job to work for myself has actually boosted my confidence and this is possibly the area in which I have seen the biggest improvement in a short space of time.

There is a lot of self-doubt and anxiety in the average freelancer's bones

And not just by a little. By a landslide.

This is how.

Space to feel confident

In a strange twist, not being around other people or having others to depend on has actually made me more confident around people. I have had to pick up the phone (I am phone phobic), chase unpaid invoices, ask for missing or late content, barter fees, present work alone when shattered on two hours' sleep and make frequent trips to meetings at offices where I knew no one or maybe only one contact in advance.

You would think the isolation makes it harder, but in a weird way I think it gives me the headspace to deal with things and work on my thought processes in the space that was usually eaten up making idle office conversation, staving off fear and paranoia, and getting stressed about things out of my control. I can now be much more purposeful about where my energies are focused and the interactions I have.

I am more confident in my work now than I have ever been. That's not to say I am supremely confident, but just quietly, contentedly confident. Sure, there are days when there is something I don't know how to do or how to fix, but I always have someone a message away who can help and I am becoming a pretty efficient Googler – finding what I need pretty darn quick.

Being assertive (and sometimes cheeky)

Rather than sit and ruminate for hours (or days) about how I am going to ask for something, push back about a demand or ask for assistance, I have to just come out with it. It might be pitching an idea, negotiating a rate or asking for something that has not been delivered. I am just me now. I can't get anyone to do it for me (except for the occasional ask of a middleman, such as a recruitment person), so I just have to deal with it. I am on the clock, and time spent working up the guts is not time paid for, so suck it up and crack on, Helen. Instead of worrying about it or feeling awkward for hours, I just get it over with. And you know what – the world doesn't implode. In fact, I have been met with respect for being efficient, knowing my stuff and being proactive. The more I do it, the more I get comfortable with it.

Though I am still rubbish at the rate negotiations. I fear that one will continue for some time.

Putting myself out there

I never thought I would have the confidence to write blog posts about myself, write for a journal, express my thoughts in a public domain, or reveal my personality. I never felt I should be 'out there'. One should be robot-like and devoid of personality at all times to remain 'business-like', right? Wrong! There are some people that still think you shouldn't do these things. These are not my people.

When I started my business, I quickly picked up on business owners who are very much themselves in their writing and promotions. I saw how it was working for them, so I started to be myself instead of a stuffy corporate machine or a fake persona. And it worked! I also started to be myself in meetings and I have had great feedback for that, with the added bonus of one of my clients remarking that he felt at ease and like he too could be himself. Win-win. That partnership is really thriving as a result and has led to three back-to-back projects from that team. And the ease we all feel shows in the work.

As a bonus-bonus, my tone of voice now finally matches my branding. My brand finally feels like me. It reflects my story, and I have the confidence to use it.

Acknowledging progress

I constantly analyse everything anyway, but I have had to learn to do this in a much more productive way. The activities in this book, particularly those at the start of part three, are my toolkit to help with this and I find them invaluable. At regular intervals, and certainly at the end of projects, I spend time looking at how I could do something better next time or maybe approach it in a different way, and what I want more or less of.

It requires stepping back and looking at things from a distance to take the personal edge out of these reflections. By reflecting on the wins and the ways of adapting in future, it gives me the confidence to move forward and keep doing what I am doing.

Giving myself a shout-out

As much as I cringe inside to do so, and I hate the whole concept of a brag, or arrogance, I have made myself start celebrating the wins. If I am feeling brave, I will give myself a public pat on the back and share my joy, whether that is just telling those close to me of my successes or putting it out there on social media. It is usually well received. Others will share in your moment. Those that don't are miserable sprouts that just need to jog on.

I started to be myself instead of a stuffy corporate machine or a fake persona

This seems especially important for us freelancers as we don't have an office of colleagues to celebrate with. It is good to share with others who understand why getting that thank you email, being paid on time, or having remembered to put the bin out in your hectic schedule are such important celebrations.

A lovely initiative started by Katie Uniacke[27] over on Instagram is #21things2021 (it started in 2020 as #20things2020 – see what she did there?), where those who want to join in post 21 lovely things to have happened each month. I use it for a combo of business and personal, and it is an interesting challenge to make yourself see and remember the positives each month. Combined with my little book of epic wins, this is a powerful way to shift your mindset and build your confidence, which also stops you hiding away all the good stuff.

Shout loud and proud.

Ask the audience

If you are having doubts or a crisis of confidence, pop on Twitter or LinkedIn and share it. Ask others how they have handled a situation. There are many like-minded lovelies who are more than willing to give advice, share their experiences, have a virtual brew together, be a sounding board, give a second opinion, or just an utterly crap joke. The camaraderie, or a well-timed GIF, can give you a surprising boost of fierceness, or a rocket up the butt, whichever is needed. It can help you to see you are not alone, and are certainly not messing up, doing things wrong or the first to experience the problem. Chances are whatever you are experiencing is a common, if not daily, occurrence among the self-employed.

Realising the successes are my own

If there was ever a confidence booster, this is it.

As someone who is abysmal at taking compliments, this is a weird one. But when something has gone right ... I have had to start acknowledging that I did that. It was my work. No one else did it. No one else can take credit. There is no middle management to take the compliment as their own or pass on a half-hearted thanks. No sneaky colleague to claim it as their own.

I need to stop making excuses for why it was good. Why I did my job well. Why it was wise to hire me. (Bloody Nora, just soak up the compliment and run with it, woman.)

Jo highlights how this has been a huge change for her too. "Working for myself has made me stretch myself to reach my full potential, rather than being

Chances are whatever you are experiencing is a common, if not daily, occurrence among the self-employed

stretched by someone else to hit someone else's targets and fulfil someone else's dreams. I like the fact that when I'm successful in achieving something, the credit, plaudits and financial rewards all come right to me!"

This is also echoed by Sophie, who says, "It's a rollercoaster, for sure. In some ways it's been easier and in some ways it's been harder. But in hindsight I've even enjoyed the hard bits because they make you stronger and you're doing it for you."

Okay, so we have to accept the mistakes too, but as we saw earlier, that I am more comfortable with.

So, let's take a look next at two things that are a swine for eroding confidence and giving us doubts – the dreaded imposter syndrome and comparisonitis. Though they present in varying degrees, for the majority they will both rear their head at some time. Possibly frequently. But the good news is that there are things you can do to stave off both of these beasts.

OVER TO YOU

How would you rate your self-confidence at the moment, out of 10?

....

At what times in the past have you been confident? Why do you think you felt more confident then?

....
....
....
....

In which areas of the business (and personally) do you need to develop your confidence most? In which areas do you feel you have more confidence and can build on this?

....
....
....
....

Which is your priority for improvement right now? Write some ideas for how you think you can action this.

....
....
....
....

AN IMPOSTER IN MY OFFICE

"If you show up with integrity and teach what you know with a lot of heart, you won't feel like an imposter."
Denise Duffield-Thomas[28]

For those who aren't familiar with it, imposter syndrome is the name attributed to when we feel like we are not good enough, like we are going to 'get found out'. That someone somewhere is going to point at and ridicule us any moment now for even thinking we were worthy of this job, dress, handbag, friendship group, amazing project, promotion…

In the report, the "State of the Workplace"[29], it was found that 96 per cent have experienced imposter syndrome and 53 per cent admitted to turning down opportunities because of a lack of confidence. So, it is no surprise that imposter syndrome seems to be one of the biggest challenges in self-employment.

Maybe it is because you are the face of your company – for everything. You have to take on things you aren't necessarily comfortable with (pitching, budget, finances, marketing, project management, and so on) as well as the work. Plus, everything comes back at you – the good comments, the bad, the queries, the grilling. And it is hard not to take these things personally when you are the only person involved.

As a rule, freelancers are very passionate about what they do and can often set very high standards for themselves. We can struggle to think 'that is enough' or 'that will do'. Plus, you don't have colleagues sat by you to bounce ideas off or a manager to check in with as to whether the work is 'good enough'. It is a personal judgement call.

Perhaps it is also because there are a high number of self-employed people who have had bad experiences in employment and have been led to believe very negative things about themselves. Just sayin'.

Whatever the reason, the rate of imposter syndrome is definitely high, so if you do get it, know you are definitely not alone.

You may watch people in wonder. Admiring how they are so comfortable being themselves and seem to have it all sussed. Seeing their amazing work and visibility. They don't get imposter syndrome, right?

Enter Jo...

"How I feel about things and how I approach things differs wildly on any given day. I'm triggered by everything from imposter syndrome to social media comparisons, and I get really fucked off whenever I have my time wasted or my value questioned by people who would probably never work with me anyway. I just deal with each day as it comes, and face each challenge one by one."

You may watch people in wonder. Admiring how they are so comfortable being themselves and seem to have it all sussed

How can we tame the monster and turn it into a soft fluffy bunny?

Here are some of the things that have helped me to lock my monster in the cupboard, at least some of the time.

- Engage in communities, find a buddy in your field (or another – that can still work) with whom you can check each other's work, bounce ideas off and brainstorm.
- Keep a folder of social media proof, a book of wins and the other celebration tips I shared at the start of the book.

- Don't be afraid to question your clients about things too. It is not a one-way street.
- Recognise your self-talk chatter – how does it start? What do you tell yourself?
- Don't be afraid to say you don't know something, need time to think or to research something.
- Share your experiences! Please, do it. You will find others have been where you are and that you are far from alone.

Hopefully, as you gain confidence, the chatter will reduce, or at least change in severity. When you have identified the chatter, take some time to sit and think what evidence there is that this is true, and maybe ask someone else's input. I'll bet you can't find a smidge of evidence.

OVER TO YOU

Start to record the self-talk when you notice it, and what
caused it. Is it always when you are in the same situation
(for example, a meeting or presentation or made to
speak up in front of people)? You are likely to spot some
recurring themes that will help you to identify your priority
areas to work on for building your confidence.

....

....

....

....

....

As you record, take time to think about whether there
really is ANY evidence to back up the feeling.

....

....

....

....

....

What action can you take to scare off the monster and turn
it into a fluffy bunny?

....

....

....

....

....

BANQUET OR BEANS

This wouldn't be a book about self-employment if the joys of the feast or famine see-saw weren't mentioned. The feast and famine cycle refers to the ups and downs in which any business finds itself; however, this can have more impact when you are a business of one relying just on yourself. It is the weeks of constant stress and overwhelm when you are juggling projects like a circus pro, only for it to come crashing down in a lull of epic tumbleweeds a couple of weeks later.

These extremes can be stressful in differing ways. It can mean the difference between a weekend fuelled by Prosecco and meals out or living on beans for a week/month. It can mean hardly seeing your family and having to work evenings and weekends one week, to not knowing what you are going to do with yourself and pestering your partner to breaking point the next (not guilty).

"Your next client is never more than two weeks away" – Giles

The best thing that can be done for your mindset in this respect is to prepare yourself for the possibility that the famine is around the corner when things are going well. That isn't to say be pessimistic and all gloomy, but just to keep a level head, and don't get carried away when the work is flooding in.

Giles has a refreshing way of viewing these tumbleweed moments. Over the years there have been fallow periods where the amount of work coming in dropped and, at the worst point, he worried that the business wasn't viable. Thankfully, things picked up quickly after that and he has a refreshing view on the familiar feast or famine cycle: "Client churn is inevitable, but I take the view that your next client is never more than two weeks away."

There is a balance to be found in making sure you don't panic when times are quiet and in taking too much on. The skill is in learning how to deal with the inevitable fluctuations and in having a strategy for how you will prioritise in busy times, and planning and preparing in the fallow times.

There are five key ways in which you can prepare yourself for this inconsistency.

1. **Don't panic when it happens (the high or the low)**
   It is not just when work is quiet we panic. Having a lot on is also stressful – the juggling of deadlines, expectations, and demands all contributes to stress levels. Make sure you maintain your boundaries and don't let clients add to the stress with moving deadlines and endless amends. Keep calm, manage their expectations, and if you can, outsource tasks to a VA or associate.

2. **Use the quiet periods to work on the business**
   Have a list of tasks to complete if and when you do experience a lull – you know, those things for ourselves and the business that we continually put off but loom on the to-do list for months, if not years. Tasks such as updating your website or portfolio – or even your CV if you still need/ use – applying for a speaking gig, scoping some podcast appearances, attending networking, putting together a passive product, learning a new skill that is in demand in your industry, applying for an award, or refreshing existing skills.

   Alternatively, prepare a load of blog posts and social media content for the next few weeks – all the things that will go to the bottom of the queue when the madness ramps up again.

NEW ASCENT. NEW RULES.

3. **Keep your visibility high, even when you are booked up with work. Don't wait for the famine to restart the campaign**

   Those materials you have prepared for point two – get them out in the world. Repurpose, repurpose, repurpose. Schedule. Enlist help. And don't forget that you will need to spare some time for engaging on these posts to keep the visibility high. Gotta love those algorithms.

4. **Learn to say no**

   If you are fully booked, don't keep taking more on 'just in case' it all goes quiet. You will end up with a crazy amount of work on and struggling to fit it all in, which could lead to burnout. I have learnt from experience. I may even be the master of this.

5. **Prepare yourself financially**

   Make sure you put some money aside each month for any months where income drops and you may need to balance it out, or to pay for any big expenditures you have coming up.

I also withdraw my dividends and then put them in a separate account, and pay myself a 'wage' from them. This means I know roughly how many months' pay I have left from this, not taking into account larger chunks or savings I have put away. I have to do this as I am terrible with money and can spend it on quite the whim, so this gives me peace of mind and one less thing to stress about each month. Treat yourself like an employee in this respect and keep it quite structured and controlled.

Other self-employed folk manage the money stuff with much more success than I do and it is a conversation that comes up fairly frequently. I have heard people say they put 10 or 20 per cent of every 'wage' into a separate account just to pay for corporation tax (something I have just started after hearing this), or pay money into National Savings as the money they get back is better than the shockingly non-existent interest rates of banks at the moment. (Next on my list to try.)

Money management really is not my forte, so I ask and learn from others, and they give me ideas that would never occur to me. Plus, it saves me hours and hours of boring research into options. Ask people in your network what they do and see what the best approach for you is to pilfer. Having that 'security' of knowing you have X month's money as a plan B is worth every penny.

Basically, it is about having some forethought and planning ahead, which are skills you need for running your own business anyway. But in order to fully live the banquet life, you also need to master the tricky skill of pricing, so let's take a look at that confidence-battering, wobbly-knees-inducing process next.

OVER TO YOU

Famine to feast: What plans can you put in place to plan for the famine?

- Put a certain percentage of your earnings each month into a separate account?
- Pay yourself a set wage?
- What will you work on in quiet periods?

....
....
....
....
....
....

Note down your plan and when you need to take those actions. (I have a note in my diary on the last Friday of every month to remind me to check the status of everything and move money around.)

SHOW ME THE MONEY!

Though this falls under the confidence banner, money confidence is an area I see self-employed people struggle with every day and so needs a chapter all of its own. This may be something that some of us will never be entirely comfortable with, but there are ways to start progressing and charging our worth.

Firstly, don't try to second-guess what your customers think, how much money they have or how much time they have for the project. You will drive yourself crazy and go in endless circles. For a start, they will usually always underestimate this to try and get a cheaper rate, but also it is not up to them to decide how long a piece of work will take to create. And we have no idea what projects they have in, or their outgoing costs, and therefore no possible way of knowing how much they have to spend.

You have to decide what is right for you and present that. Tell them what you need, how much you are worth and what fabulousness you give them for their dosh. If you can explain everything you offer that adds value, then you will find they rarely quibble. Or at least barter a little less.

> "'Charge your worth' doesn't mean your worth as a human. No one can afford that. Calm down."
> **Laura Belgray, *Talking Shrimp*[30]**

There does appear to be something of a gender bias when it comes to money too. Us ladies are letting our self-doubts undervalue ourselves. The IPSE (the Association of Independent Professionals and the Self-Employed)[31] have found that self-employed men earn 43 per cent more than women, which is significantly higher than the 17 per cent difference among employees. C'mon ladies, let's give the boys a run for their money!

If all else fails, I'm going to have to insist we adopt Penny Brazier's[32] idea: "Life would be sweeter if every time I realized I had drastically underquoted for a project, a marching band burst into my office and played 'Oops I did it again' and we had a little dance."

Self-employed men earn 43 per cent more than women

My lightbulb moment on charging my worth was someone pointing out that customers aren't just paying for my time right here right now for this project. They are paying for my years of experience. For the skills I have developed that allow me to complete the work in a shorter space of time. Why would you knock your rates down (and essentially punish yourself) for having developed this skill? Why should someone with less experience and skill be paid more as they take longer to do it?

I can't remember which sage originally said this to me, but it is something that Emma Cownley discusses too in her *Kiss My A's* series. I particularly recommend checking out *How to price a freelance project (PROPERLY!)* over on her YouTube channel.[33] In fact, check her out for tips on all many aspects of running your own business. She is one wisdomous freelancer, and her videos are pure gold.

There is so much conflicting advice out there when it comes to what to charge and whether to do it by hour, the day, the project or the outcome, so as a start, you need to do some exploratory work to see what is the norm in your industry (if there is one). You may also be dictated somewhat by whether you are working directly with clients or through agencies.

By making sure you charge your worth and by regularly upping your rates, you give yourself more free time or time to work on your business and side projects. It also means you are not having to constantly up the number of hours worked each year to increase the amount you bring home. A lesson I have learnt at my peril.

Tips for charging your worth

If you really hate the money talk, there are a few tips I have picked up along the way which may help you.

- Make sure you can articulate the value you offer! Go in there with your arguments formed, and believe them.

> *Make sure you can articulate the value you offer!*

- Practise saying your rate to someone else – or even just yourself around the house. Once you have said aloud "That's £xxxx", it might start to feel a little less scary. In fact, practise an amount higher than you are going to charge, then your figure will seem less daunting to say aloud or in writing.
- If you are quoting verbally, have it written in front of you. For some reason I find this makes me less likely to suddenly shout out a much lower fee.
- Have a stock response for if they try to barter. This comes back to understanding and being able to communicate your value. Instead of being talked down you could go with an alternative response of "I can do that fee but it means taking X out of the project".
- Regularly review and increase your rates! Commit to doing it at least once a year, or more frequently in smaller increments.
- Remember, clients are not just paying you for your time and resources now, they are paying you for all your years of experience that mean you can get the work done quickly and professionally. Keep in mind the old adage "Pay cheap, pay twice".
- If you have no idea where to start and want to get a good understanding of the options for pricing, I recommend buying the *Work Notes Freelance Pricing Guide*.[34] It is a

bargain of a resource that will bring you more money in the long run. Much sterling advice in there.

- Check out the work of Denise Duffield-Thomas around money blocks – in particular, her book *Get Rich, Lucky Bitch* or her Money Bootcamp. (Disclaimer: I haven't read this book nor am I a member of the bootcamp but they come highly recommended and I like her other book, *Chillpreneur* – despite my aversion to all things 'preneur.)

I'm off to practise what I preach...

Prepare some responses for when bartering situations arise. How will you push back?

....
....
....
....
....
....
....
....

Write a list of why you are worth your rate – the skills, experience and knowledge you bring – and why that means your rate is what it is.

....
....
....
....
....
....
....
....
....

IS IT BEAUTIFUL ENOUGH FOR YOU?

"Confidence isn't walking into a room with your nose in the air, and thinking you are better than everyone else. It's walking into a room and not having to compare yourself with anyone in the first place."
Digital Women[35]

This seems as good a point as any to bring up the beast to which we all fall prey now and again – comparisonitis. The beast that usually rears its ugly head when you are already feeling wobbly, having a bad day, feeling stressed and hopeless, or your resilience is on a landslide, it pops up to make you feel like everyone else is winning at life and you're ... definitely not.

It usually comes to the forefront on days where we find ourselves procrastinating and doom scrolling on social media – when we spot friends, business connections, or even random strangers and find ourselves musing at some success they have, or wonder why we cannot have it as good as them. When we wonder just how they have built this miraculously, easy-breezy freelance life.

I have certainly been sucked into the depths of comparisonitis before, particularly when at my lowest ebb. I would look around the office and see how others were getting promotions, good feedback, or even just being invited to lunches that I wasn't, and I'd get myself worked up. The more I got stressed and felt left behind, the more I compared, and so I got even more stressed and upset. That is a cycle no one needs to be in.

If you leave the beast to take control in this way for too long, this mindset can be significantly detrimental to your mental health and confidence, increase your stress levels and anxiety, and make you feel more and more of a failure, outcast, or insert your own word of choice here. The beast will throw you in that room, lock the door, glue you to the seat, and set you ruminating over and over where you went wrong.

The challenge here is to spot when you are slipping into comparison behaviours, and why. We do it all the time, and in small amounts it can be fine: it can keep our motivations high, or provide inspiration. Who hasn't had a good nosy at old schoolfriends' houses on Facebook, looked up what jobs our contacts are doing on LinkedIn and stalked their Instagram feeds for their latest holiday destinations?

When it feeds into other issues and creates unproductive behaviours, negative emotions and makes you feel worthless, it is certainly time to stop.

The legend that is Glennon Doyle captures this perfectly in *Untamed*: "The truth is that it matters not at all what you think of my life - but it matters supremely what you think of your own... You are not here to waste your time deciding whether my life is true and beautiful enough for you. You are here to decide if your life, relationships, and world are true and beautiful enough for you."[36]

Who hasn't had a good nosy at old schoolfriends' houses on Facebook?

Bingo!

When you notice comparison behaviours, take a step back and remind yourself that you have no idea of what is going on in that person's life. Sometimes, this is the case, even if you know them well. You are seeing a small snippet. The tip of the iceberg. Such a small part of their day, not even one per cent. And it has been carefully selected and curated to share.

Remember that most often people only show the positive aspects of their lives, the stuff they think sounds impressive or bragworthy, particularly when it comes to business. You may be seeing an award they've won, but you are not seeing the blood, sweat and tears that led to the victory. You may be seeing the end result of a project, but you are not seeing the exhausting pitching process they went through, the late nights working and the vat of sugar needed to power them through. You may see them leading a great team, but you are not seeing the loneliness they feel, trapped in an office and no longer invited on team social occasions.

This is why I feel it is important to be authentic on social media – to show your highs and your lows. Let others see 'behind the scenes,' to see that you do, in fact, lose customers and fail to win projects sometimes, that you have rollercoaster weeks of both fabulous moments and those where you're crying into your (probably cold) brew and only have stale biscuits to comfort eat as you haven't been to the shop all week. Or, in my case, that your head is elsewhere and it has just taken you seven hours to realise you had odd slippers on. (True story, but I rocked the look.) The lows can make the highs all the sweeter.

I also find that these posts are the ones that get the most engagement on social media as so many people relate, so they can also help your visibility. I have had clients tell me that my honesty and authenticity is why they chose me for projects, along with my sharing of industry knowledge and skills. I may be more worried if they chose me purely due to my inability to match slippers.

In the same way, we should also not compare ourselves to other people's perceived failures. Steve Morgan explains this implication I had not considered before, in his book *Anti-Sell: Marketing, Lead Generation and Networking Tips for Freelancers Who Hate Sales.*[37] "Other people's failures are other people's failures, not yours. So when people talk about the survival rate of freelancers, small businesses and startups, just remember: if other people fail, that doesn't mean you will too."

There's some wisdom right there.

How to stop doom scrolling

Here are my top tips to get you out of the comparison scroll.

1. To prevent doom scrolling behaviours, open your social media feed, swipe three finger scrolls down, work your way back up the feed from there, then close the app down. This stops you going to infinity, losing hours and exposing yourself to hundreds of stories from others.

2. Move your social media apps to the last menu screen on your phone or a folder. This one has worked fantastically for me – truly out of sight out of mind. If you are not seeing the little number of notifications tick up or being reminded by the little app image, you'll pick it up less over time.

3. Turn off your notifications. Make a boundary to check your social media on your own terms, at times that work for you.

The short story – do not compare yourself to someone else's filtered one per cent. Whether that be good or bad. Your story is your story. Go own it.

OVER TO YOU

Can you think of any examples of comparative thinking you have displayed lately? Where you have compared yourself unfavourably to someone else? Or made an assumption about someone's life from the small snippet you have seen?

....

....

....

....

....

Next time you are in the office, a public space or on social media, notice what internal monologue you have going on. Try to catch and change these thought patterns; journal on them if you need to. A good exercise is to record how many times in a day you catch yourself and see if you can bring it down over time.

....

....

....

....

....

....

HOME ALONE

My chap's initial reaction on being told I was going to be working from home was, quite rightly, along the lines of, "Oh good God! This can't end well."

The thought of sitting at home alone all day is, admittedly, one of the things that had put me off freelancing full time. I am a prolifically restless person and, in the past, I have often suffered from terrible cabin fever, even just being in the house for a full weekend, which saw me dragging Graham out here, there and everywhere. We were both expecting that he would come home within a matter of days (or hours) to find me rocking in a corner, trying to claw my way out of the door with a spoon.

But it never happened.

Some days he did get a garbled torrent of musings launched his way as soon as he walked in the door, on account of me having spoken to no one all day, but that was as far as the mania went. (Ahem.)

I promptly set up an office in the spare bedroom and was given free rein to decorate how I wanted (a miracle in itself) ... and I have barely moved since. I am not sure I could ever go back to being in an office full time. I also don't get the cabin fever like I used to, which I really can't fathom. It seems to have made me embrace being at home more than I ever have before. Having the dedicated office space certainly helps.

Since going it alone I have found that I am not alone. Though I don't have colleagues, I do have a network. And I am far from lonely. There's a huge pool of people out there who feel exactly the same.

NEW ASCENT. NEW RULES.

> "One thing that was key to my success was the people
> I surrounded myself with right from the get-go. Being
> employed is guaranteed to pit you both with and against
> others, and there's a good chance you won't like everyone.
> Being self-employed gifts you the ability to surround
> yourself with people you actually want to work and spend
> time with, and it's bloody liberating!"
> **Joelle**

But not all freelancers are managing to banish the loneliness. In
2018, research by Epson[38] found that 48 per cent of freelancers
said their job makes them feel lonely, and 46 per cent said it
is isolating. In contrast, there are those who find they prefer
interaction with 3D humans, and the rise of co-working spaces
is helping them to find the environment that works for them. A
Harvard Business Review survey[39] found that 83 per cent of people
said they feel less lonely working in co-working environments
and 89 per cent said they are happier since joining a co-working
space. Then there are the people who like the hubbub of working
in coffee shops or the calm of libraries. Sarah Townsend,
author of *Survival Skills for Freelancers*, often works in the café
of her gym.

Social media is not just about pushing out your content, it is about building a community

Whether you use these other options
or not, the online networks are here
to stay and such a superb source of
connection that I recommend everyone
get involved in them.

Social media is not just about pushing
out your content, it is about building a
community, a network, relationships
– both with clients and friends. It
is supporting one another, sharing
insights and inspiration, and generating ideas. We bounce off one
another; we build one another.

As a group, we are battered and bruised, fragile, and find it hard to forget prior experiences, but, having taken control, we are building successful businesses and a life we could only have imagined for a long time. We are stronger. And we are winning contracts from under the noses of the corporate giants. How? Because we care, we have passion, we're fuelled by self-development and we provide the personal touch. And clients are listening, They prefer this way of working. They are realising that freelancers and contractors are the future of work, and not just because it also generally works out cheaper for them. They prefer to interact with a human rather than a faceless robot. They prefer to be able to deal directly with the person actually doing the work rather than layers of managers and project managers.

There are so many networks out there for business owners that it is actually hard to be alone. I have made more friends in the last two years than I probably have in my life. Admittedly, I have only met a few face-to-face (thanks again, pandemic), but I certainly will meet more. Plans are already in place. In the last 12 months alone I have had calls with people in the UK, Europe and the USA. Just for a brew, a chinwag, to put the world to rights, to share common interests. No ulterior motives involved.

The rise of digital conferences and online networks has also helped many who would otherwise have felt exhausted purely by the thought of face-to-face networking, like Giles.

> "Being able to network virtually through the Federation of Small Businesses (FSB) and Freelance Heroes has given me the opportunity to meet new people from all over the UK, not just the North West or North Midlands. Virtual networking is much less demanding for me than face-to-face meetings, both in terms of the logistics, time and effort involved, and the drain on my mental and physical resources. As an introvert and Aspie (Asperger's) male, I find social interactions draining, whereas extroverts are energised by them."

In the many channels I have joined (see my favourites in the resources section), there are formal chats, informal chats, biscuit and brew time, accountability sessions, training, rant chats, pet chats, inspiration chats, book clubs, morning check-ins, wellness tips, pleas for help, and whatever else you can shake your post-its at. And all of them go answered. Not a tumbleweed in sight, no shouting into the void.

You can reach out for anything.

Bored? Tell them.

Feeling crap. Share it.

Stuck for ideas? They've got loads of the things.

Technology failing you? Someone knows someone who knows stuff.

Something to celebrate? They've got the fizz and GIFs ready.

Your dog doing something cute or your cat something stupid? Take a pic and post it; someone will love it.

At the end of a recent two-day conference with Freelance Heroes, a fabulous comment was made by Sharon Gray, a fellow freelancer, who had so far hung out on the edge of our community and not engaged much. Over those two days she realised how much she had been missing.

> "Now that I've spent two days listening to your speakers, spending time meeting people and chatting in the breakout rooms, I've got a different view of Freelance Heroes; you've all turned into real people, some with the same problems as me. I now see you as a real community of warm, lovely supportive people – and not just another Facebook group."[40]

The value of these communities is not to be sniffed at, and the more you put in, the more you get out. It is worth the time investment. Far from being competitors, the freelance community are colleagues, collaborators, maybe even co-conspirators. They are a weapon in giving you referrals, passing on projects they don't have the capacity or skills for, sharing your work, and more. Matthew says, "One of my biggest challenges is finding regular work. We all want a quick fix; the fact is, there isn't one. It takes years of showing up and building relationships to get regular work that earns you a living."

Just don't spread yourself too thin. I ended up in so many groups that the constant notifications, even when muted, became a source of stress as I constantly felt like I had so much to catch up on. It just adds to the to-do list.

Better to be in one or two communities and engage fully than never really build the quality connections

Don't forget that in building your presence on social media platforms, such as LinkedIn, you will also build a network there – and those are not ones to be dropped (unless your clients aren't on there...), so bear in mind you'd be adding networks and communities on top of existing profiles to manage.

By being everywhere, it means you risk missing out on building proper connections in a few well-selected areas. It also means that what would be five minutes mindless scrolling on one page, ends up being an hour across five or six. Nobody needs that. It takes some serious discipline to not let that level of notification madness affect your workflow.

So, I had a group-cull. I only kept those groups where I felt I could give and get the most from. Better to be in one or two communities and engage fully than never really build the quality connections. Those where you are comfortable and find value are priceless. I have found some real keepers, and people that I would now call friends. People who understand the challenge of your business threatening to take over your life, the long hours and juggling with other responsibilities, not being able to take time off if you don't set those boundaries and schedule properly, the awkwardness of pitching and pricing, the fact that the business cannot just grind to a halt, even if you need it to while you deal with something else that life has thrown at you.

Even if they don't have any suggestions of help, they will have a very supportive ear, check in on how you are doing, have your back and do anything they can to help, and even send cards and gifts to perk you up. I have never seen people pay it forward as much as I have in the freelance groups. It is something of an unspoken covenant: that you do it for others, and if you ever need it, you know for sure they will too.

Them peeps have got your back.

> "Quite simply, I couldn't have gotten to where I've … er, gotten to without the help of my competitors. I've learned a huge amount over the years from other people in the same field. And I've been blown away by the openness and generosity.
>
> My competitors have been my greatest referrers and my best customers. And most importantly, I now consider many of them to be my best friends."
> **Kate Toon, *Confessions of a Misfit Entrepreneur*[41]**

Look into the networks available to you (check my list in the resources section for a start). Write a list of the ones you think you'd like to try out.

....

....

....

....

....

....

Engagement is key – so set some time aside each day or week to start interacting and giving to others, to build relationships. When could you find the time to interact in them? Is there a timeslot you could set aside to do so?

....

....

....

....

....

....

A HOUSE IS NOT JUST A HOME...

... It's an office, warehouse, distribution centre, marketing hub, print shop and whatever other purpose it may have to fulfil.

There are two key points to think about if you are going to be working from home in self-employment: what space you need to run your business; and how you can make the most of being at home all day every day while keeping the work-home life boundaries.

For my business, I just need me, my laptop, an extra monitor and a desk. Just before I went solo we had recently moved to a bigger house (to actually be nearer my workplace ... whoops! I haven't lived that one down yet), so I knew I had the space to be able to create a designated workspace, even with my sizeable book, craft and stationery haul. If you have a business selling products, holding events, or which requires lots of equipment, there are extra considerations for how you set up working from home.

I have absolutely relished being at home full time.

- To no longer have to commute for two to three hours a day.
- To be able to cook proper lunches.
- To have a lie-in if my insomnia strikes in the night.
- To be able to control my working environment and noise levels – to an extent at least (my neighbours' serious STIHL saw habit and barking dogs aside).
- To be able to listen to whatever music I like, or even have a film on in the background.
- To be able to move and do my physio exercises throughout the day.

But something that became abundantly clear very quickly is that I am not good at separating my home life and work life. Due to the combination of being something of a workaholic, pushing myself too hard, and my home being my workspace, it is easier than ever to 'just do a bit more' every day, to let the work creep into evenings and weekends, and it is harder to switch off from thinking about my work. This has led to a couple of episodes of tipping into burnout and I have had to learn to be very strict with myself. This is something I will have to continually work at for the foreseeable. Even taking this into consideration, I can't ever see myself heading back into an office. I don't see this challenge as a negative of working from home, just something I need to be aware of and manage.

I suspect this is the case for a lot of business owners, especially when you first start out and want to hit the ground running. It is only once you start to see a steady stream of work or orders that you feel a bit more able to take your foot off the gas.

Don't get me wrong, there are some downsides to working from home. I am just yet to find any significant ones. My more trivial findings are as follows.

- I miss wearing jewellery and 95 per cent of my wardrobe – jeans and hoodies all the way.
- I get little in the way of exercise and fresh air (yes, I know I am making excuses for being a lazy git here).
- I have gained a new unexpected role – postmaster general for the estate. Those delivery men soon suss out who is at home every day.
- I never have the foggiest what day it is; everything merges into one when you have no change of scenery.
- If you ain't got the brew and biscuits in, ain't no one got the biscuits in: a freelancer's worst nightmare.
- The employed think it means you do sod all. That you have ALL the time for chores and shopping, doing favours for others, unannounced drop-ins on your doorstep, play dates, long ladies-that-lunch type shenanigans, babysitting your neighbour's child/dog/sick cat … and so on.

However, I think you will agree most of these can be resolved with a bit of planning or a few stern words. The positives outweigh the negative niggles by far. (Admittedly, I did not foresee the change the pandemic would bring – having t'other half at home every day now too. Permanently.)

You might not have control over, or choice of, some things, but by planning out your space and time, and hopefully making a designated workspace, you will provide yourself the best opportunity to get your head in the right space.

If you do start to feel lonely, at least you know your friendly local delivery man will soon be knocking with your neighbour's next parcel and you can talk his ear off. If he's not too busy poking fun at the frequency of your wine deliveries...

Do you have the space to bring your work into your home without it being claustrophobic? If not, how could you create the space?

....

....

....

....

....

....

Would you have to share an office space with your partner if they also work from home?

....

....

....

....

....

....

Will your business require more than just a laptop and space to work? Do you need space to store merchandise, or a studio area for making your products?

....

....

....

....

....

....

Do you have kiddiewinks home all or part of the day, which will affect your work abilities and concentration?

....

....

....

....

....

....

How will you maintain the boundaries between work and home life?

....

....

....

....

....

....

CAN'T PUT A PRICE ON THAT

Business values are the (often unspoken) beliefs and principles that guide your work, behaviour and interactions. They are the values that complement your mission and ethics. They are what give you purpose and clarity. They underpin and guide your business.

I highly recommend you have a list of values and that you have them in the open, from day one, if not before. When there are many others out there who do what you do, communicating your values can help you stand out and make you more relatable. It will make tasks like pitching and deciding your boundaries so much easier.

The starting point for creating my business values derived from my previous experiences in employment. I left employment with a strong sense of what I thought was right or wrong for me and my future clients. I had a clear view of how I thought people should be treated and the way to get the best work out of me. I had a good idea of the type of projects that are best for me. There were causes I cared about but I didn't get to pursue. Most of all, I knew there was a way I needed to work to achieve happiness and calm.

I left employment with a strong sense of what I thought was right or wrong for me and my future clients

As a result, I formalised my values for UnlikelyGenius™, which at time of writing are these.

- **Learning**
  I continually strive to develop my skills and knowledge and to share my learning with others in my network and beyond. I aim to create an environment where people are excited by learning.

- **The learners/audiences**
  Living by my mantra 'The content you create is not for you', I believe the end user should be the focus of the design experience, not our personal preferences as designers, CEO, marketing, anyone else with an opinion.
- **Flexibility**
  A significant factor in why I went into self-employment – I thrive on flexibility and also allow my clients flexibility to fit around their needs.
- **Make it easy**
  Why overcomplicate things? I guide clients through the process and make projects easy to manage. I explain the technicalities in plain language. No flouncy fluff (bunnies aside) and jarring jargon here. I bring experience from a range of disciplines and work on the full process so clients only need to hire one person instead of multiple.
- **Openness and authenticity**
  I am who I am. I will no longer be pushed down or forced to be someone else. I allow those who work with me this freedom too. No pretence or arrogance here. Just a clumsy buffoon.
- **Creativity**
  Creativity is at the core of everything I do and I help my clients to have a more creative approach to their work. Exploration, trial and error and making mistakes are all welcome here.
- **Community and supporting one another**
  I continue to be active in communities and networks where we support one another, and will continue to provide resources to help others. In particular, I will help new and existing freelancers to establish themselves, and families looking to become more sustainable. I will be establishing my own communities for these too.
- **Happiness**
  I will set boundaries to help prevent overwhelm and stress, and aim to take on work that excites me and brings me joy.

Likewise, I aim to make the lives of my clients easier and stress-free through their dealings with me, and to have fun.

- **The planet, the oceans, creatures great and small**
  I will take continual steps towards becoming a more sustainable business, to protect our wildlife and lessen my negative impacts on the world. Plus, through our Be The Future project, I will continue to help educate the next generation and their families about looking after our planet.

- **Which leads me onto, of course ... The Bunnies**
  AKA my assistants (ahem, bosses). I shall continue to work hard to keep them in the life to which they have become accustomed, and the expensive parsley to which they are partial. (They are the very reason I need clients to pay on time.)

Why create a values list?

> "Your values are a continual career compass to guide your decisions and actions."
> **Helen Tupper and Sarah Ellis, *The Squiggly Career*[42]**

When you make the leap, you may find that your attitude to work changes, and you see work in a totally different light. Therefore, your values will change too, as Craig found. "Self-employment has changed my outlook. I'm far more helpful when working for myself and have a determination to do a good job and keep my customers happy. I didn't have that so much as an employee, as I was given less to do, and had to follow their working practices and make more compromises than I'm comfortable with. Self-employment is more rewarding too, financially and emotionally."

Instead of hiding your values away, live by them, communicate by them

This shows how the values work two ways too. A happier worker leads to a happier client. You will probably find more things you value when working for yourself than you did working for others, because you have the forum to do so. Your values are not being directed by those of a team in a boardroom. You'd never have seen bunnies appear on the values list of any company I've worked for.

Instead of hiding your values away, look at the changes you have experienced and what is now important to you, and use them to yours and your clients' advantage. Live by them, communicate by them. Use them to tell your story, giving purpose to your communications and interactions. Explain your interpretation of them.

> "Identifying your values is incredibly important but it's just as important to be able to define what you mean by each value. You need to be able to share what a value means to you, otherwise it's easy for other people to put their own interpretation on your words."
> **Helen Tupper and Sarah Ellis, *The Squiggly Career*[43]**

Businesses with a clear purpose and mission are much more relatable and appealing. There has been a significant increase in employees looking to work with businesses that care about things like sustainability and mental health. A Reuters survey[44] found that almost two-thirds (65 per cent) of survey respondents said that they were more likely to work for a company with strong environmental policies. Climate change, human rights and social equity are all issues of growing importance, especially for millennial employees, who now make up the majority of the workforce.

Ultimately, values have an important role to play in increasing your confidence, showing the real you behind the business, and can impact how you promote your business and the projects you take on. They may even carve out a niche for you. For example, I would not take on a project for a fossil fuel company as this is against my value of looking after the environment. I am also looking to carve out more opportunities to work in sustainability and with organisations that are playing their part in protecting the planet. It increases your chances of attracting like-minded clients.

Self-employment brought about a huge change for Pavitra in the form of an increase in her self-confidence and being herself, living to her values. "An important aspect of self-employment is not putting up a pretence. Whatever the business, the way you conduct it reflects who you are as a person. Your business is a mirror projecting the inner workings of your mind and there is nowhere to hide!"

As they grew, Feasts & Fables (check out their content: they are awesome) went one step further and took their values and made them into The Encouragement Manifesto.[45] This manifesto is made up of ten values which one hundred per cent show the essence of their company, and the way they carry out their work. It shows their priorities, honesty, even their vulnerability. It shows their positivity, and love of community. And above all else it shows authenticity ... an essential trait for anyone looking to communicate their values.

> "When we ran a small business, there were values at its heart. It was owner-run; just the two of us. So the way we worked, who we were, was never written down as such. It was in our hearts. We are pretty sure it was clear to our customers who we were and what was important to us. We worked hard to be consistent, to celebrate others and to stay positive and optimistic.

> Our business was built on the successes and strengths of others; kindness and generosity were keystones. We only talked about value, not price; slowly, gently, we built a community. We gathered up and shared inspiring stories and we sought to be a pebble in the pond, creating ripples. These values are now at the heart of The Encouragement Manifesto."

Amazing work.

Often when it comes to the values of a business, owners and staff can sometimes vaguely recite a couple of points if asked, but many companies don't write them down or formalise them. Then there are certainly some companies who do it for lip service and don't actually live by them. You see it time and time again with companies that roll out the banners for Mental Health Day, Pride or other 'causes' once a year, then pack it all away and carry on as they were. Don't be one of these people: you will get found out, and that will do nothing for your credibility and reputation.

So, where should you start?

Even if you can't articulate your values right now or don't feel they are in reach yet, think about where you would like to be. Tim Denning[46] says, "It's not where you are right now but where you're heading that determines your value."

Start with listing some thoughts under the question prompts provided here. It can just be single words for now. You can expand on them later when you have decided on the final ones you want to take forward and that matter the most to you. Take your time, and keep coming back to this one.

Note: If you would like more help in deciding on your values, I recommend taking a look at chapter two of *The Squiggly Career* (see recommended resources), which provides a framework for helping you to define them.

OVER TO YOU

What were your reasons for making the leap? How could these inform your values?

....
....
....
....
....

What is important to you in life? And are there particular causes you care about?

....
....
....
....
....

Look back to the growth you defined earlier in this section. Are there any points which could complement or be influenced by the points you made there?

....
....
....
....
....

AN OPEN BOOK (ISH)

> "I've never been one of those people with an 'at work'
> professional personality and an 'at home' personality.
> Maybe that was part of the problem?"
> **Craig**

Hard relate.

The first time someone told me they liked my authenticity I was
quite surprised. As I mentioned at the start of the book, I had
felt like I was having to impersonate someone else for a long
time as my real personality was not wanted in corporate land.
At the point the comment was made I hadn't fully realised quite
how much I had embraced being allowed to be myself, but I can
really see now how this is one of the biggest areas in which I have
developed. It is very freeing to be allowed to be yourself. (I would
like to add 'with no judgement' here, but let's face it, there is
always a Geoff or a Karen waiting in the social media wings with
their unsolicited 'advice'.)

Being authentic probably means different things to each of us,
but for me it is about always being true to myself, my values and
beliefs. Giving my full self to a project. Not dampening down my
personality for others. Not feeling like I have to put on a different
hat (that is, a stuffy, suffocating corporate one) to do my work.
It is about sharing my skills and knowledge with others. It is
giving to others what I also get from them (support, celebration,
commiseration, friendship, and so on). It is taking the time to
build my passions and work on passion projects.

This same sentiment is described by the lovely Sarah Townsend
in her fabulous book *Survival Skills for Freelancers*[47]: "Good
business is about authenticity and openness – and that means
being proud of who you are and what you do, rather than
pretending to be something you're not." I couldn't agree more.

It helps that this is also reflected in my business brand, UnlikelyGenius™ – the name and logo really have the essence of 'me' (especially now I have updated the brand). The self-deprecating nature, with a hint to me actually knowing my stuff, is me to a T. I have (semi-)confident moments, I have crushing imposter moments, but I always work my hardest and will deliver the goods.

In *Company of One*, Paul Jarvis discusses how the role of personality has changed.

> "Personality – the authentic you that traditional business has taught you to suppress under the guise of 'professionalism' – can be your biggest edge over the competition when you're a company of one. What's even better is that while skills and expertise can be replicated, it's damn near impossible to replicate someone's personality and style."[48]

Admittedly, authenticity is a word that seems to provoke quite a reaction at the moment. It has become a bit of a buzzword, though I have not added it to the 'bullshit bingo' list yet (the name I have given to the endless business jargon used by some people/companies; for example, blue sky thinking, touch base, low-hanging fruit), so it can't be too bad. The problem with authentic is when it is used by people who are anything but.

I have never been a fan of this 'influencer' culture, or the many strains of 'preneurs. Aside from the fact that they make me cringe, they are often self-proclaimed titles that carry a certain amount of vanity and arrogance, which does not sit well with me. They all blur into one stick-insect-like orange blur. There are those doing it well, but on the whole I find it a very fake premise, particularly when it comes to the influencers. I am certainly not all about the money, beach living and being famous for nothing, as these labels often are.

Where they are posing with the latest Louis Vuitton, hanging out in Dubai hotspots, and being draped in the latest trends, I am prancing around with my rabbits, sharing my ups and downs in any given week, being honest about my strengths and weaknesses, and regularly providing free resources and content to help others. I am showing a genuine passion for what I do. I love learning and will waffle about it until the cows come home – whether it is something I have learnt for the business, or my latest crafty hobby.

Being authentic doesn't have to mean putting all of yourself out there – after all we don't need or want to know everything. It sounds counter-intuitive with the idea of being open, but you *can* pick and choose the parts you are comfortable to show, and work towards more if it feels good. It is about finding the balance between giving enough for us to see the real you, without divulging the minutiae of your life.

> It is about finding the balance between giving enough for us to see the real you, without divulging the minutiae of your life

You may give extra glimmers in certain places – for example, I am much more open about my health issues in closed networks than in the general open ones, for example on blog posts or social media posts. Though I will hint at them, it is not something I want to talk about in detail with anyone and everyone, so I keep some information back. I may mention that I have a health issue that hinders concentration, causes issues with my eyes/muscles/balance, or that I am in pain every day and how this creates challenges in running a business, but my audience generally doesn't need to know more than that. Some say they don't need to know this information at all and we shouldn't talk about it – but as I advocate for transparency, honesty and getting rid of the shaming culture around health and well-being issues, I am happy to. It is a huge part of me and has made me who I am – it is also what made me become self-employed in the first place and is part of my story. It is my story to tell.

Similarly, Francesca is very open about her challenges with anorexia. The fact that she is so open about her eating disorder and recovery is inspiring for others. It was certainly one aspect that has drawn me to her in online communities and a reason I asked her to contribute to this book, and it is helping her to attract clients who appreciate the honesty.

And we don't share these insights for comments of "Oh, you're so brave", "How do you manage?" – though this kind of honesty does often lead to those. I tell my story as it can help others in my situation, it can make them feel less alone and it gives us all a wider network to talk to about our wonky bodies when we need the outlet. It keeps the conversation going about health in the workplace, the benefits of working for yourself, and it helps to inspire and give hope to others in the same boat.

If you want some reassurance – I have never had a negative comment about doing this either since working for myself. Only when working for others – when I was encouraged to hide it, told to get over it, told it would hinder my progress. That speaks volumes. About the employer, not me.

HERE'S ANOTHER HOME TRUTH: IF YOU TRY TO BE SOMEONE YOU'RE NOT, YOU WON'T ATTRACT YOUR KIND OF PEOPLE. SO IF YOU PUT YOURSELF OUT THERE AS SOME BIG FURRY BALLED SALES BITCH, THEN YOU'RE GOING TO ATTRACT CUSTOMERS WHO WANT THAT KIND OF ATTITUDE FROM YOU DAY IN AND DAY OUT. IT'S TRULY EXHAUSTING TRYING TO BE SOMETHING YOU'RE NOT.

KATE TOON, *CONFESSIONS OF A MISFIT ENTREPRENEUR*[49]

How can you be more authentic?

Here are some of my suggestions.

- Share your passions, and your stumbles. Your highs, your lows, your in-betweens.
- Share widely; share freely.
- Help others. Be generous with your time, brain, skills. (Note that this does not mean working for free.)
- Talk openly about your beliefs and values.
- Live to your values – write some both for your company and you as an individual if you haven't already.
- Be honest.
- Don't promise to do things you don't know how to do.
- Share your approach and processes.
- Use realistic imagery of yourself with a genuine smile (don't get me started on trout pouts) – not overly doctored, filtered, 'I made my eyes as big as a Disney princess' type photos.
- Write as you speak. Have a conversation with your audience.

A great place to start is to look at the online profiles of someone you feel is authentic – look at the types of stories they tell, their language, and how they communicate their values within the stories. When looking at them, consider what could work for you. Has it sparked any ideas of stories you might want to tell? What makes them seem authentic to you?

Next up, let's look at vulnerability as a superpower and how that will work alongside your authenticity.

OVER TO YOU

What does authenticity look like to you? Can you define it?

What makes you unique, interesting, 'you'? How can you communicate this?

In which areas do you feel you could be more authentic – how could you represent the 'true you' more online and in your work? Even if you are not comfortable and confident enough to do it yet, write down your ideas so you can have them in mind and start working towards them.

What is your 'story'? Which parts of it are you happy to tell, and where?

....
....
....
....
....
....
....
....
....
....
....
....
....
....
....
....
....
....
....
....
....
....
....

BARING ALL

Vulnerability. What a divisive topic!

It's a topic I have seen debated many a time, particularly on forums such as LinkedIn.

Should you show it?

Should you let people see the real you?

Should you let 'business connections' into your real life?

Many say yes. In this age run by social media, we need to represent our true selves and lives. That would be me. I am firmly on the yes side.

Others say no. They tend to be the stuffy corporate types with old-fashioned values. My other half is one of them as a result of over a decade in local government. (I'm in for some grief if he reads this.)

While I can regularly be seen on Zoom calls introducing the bunnies, or even making my cuddly pain au chocolat, aka 'Juan the Pain', dance across the screen, him indoors will move all his equipment for a 10-minute video call so that there is nothing behind him that relays any character or homeliness. (The plate rack with salt and pepper guinea pigs behind where he works is a huge no.) He even used to switch off the Christmas lights that were draped behind him as that wasn't professional enough for his environment.

For me, there is no hiding. No pretence. No fakeness. No corporate dryness.

I show my values, my ethics, my heart.

I try to be helpful to others in sharing my knowledge and skills widely and freely.

I have shared my frustrations at being in constant pain.

I have shared my 'ranty pants' Tuesday offloads.

I have asked for help. Especially when something has gone wrong and I needed another perspective.

I have shared my hopes and fears.

I have shared when I have been screwed over by a client.

And I have had to be vulnerable to do this – to wear my heart on my sleeve, and share experiences, home truths and lessons learnt.

It has done wonders for the business and it has contributed hugely to this book. Plus, I have had many comments from fellow freelancers to say thank you for sharing as it has helped them in some way.

Being honest and open comes with a side of vulnerability. Again, this is not a case of being one end of the scale or the other. The topic and even your mood on any given day will affect how vulnerable you are happy to be. But it is worth at least trying. Vulnerability has become associated with such negative connotations, when actually it takes great strength of character to show it.

I can't abide fakeness. If someone isn't being open and vulnerable at least a little of the time, I can be quite suspicious of that. And if someone doesn't want to work with me because I have shown vulnerability, then they are not the client for me anyway.

One argument for keeping vulnerability to yourself is the fear that others may try to take advantage of you. Firstly, it likely wouldn't have stopped them anyway. Secondly, there is a difference between being vulnerable in letting people see the ups and downs of running a business, sharing the difficulties in your industry, or giving your audience a taste of other areas of your life, and the vulnerability which I would actually class as gullibility or weakness. 'Oh yes, please, Mr Dodginess, prince of far-off lands. Let me give you all my monies to invest in your new, lucrative bitcoin business offer.'

Sometimes, vulnerability may be just asking for help. This is a huge step for many people (me included) and not something that is always easy to accept, especially when in previous experiences you would have been beaten down if you did ask for help. But my experience of asking for help in self-employment is that you will learn, develop and build more amazing connections. No one preys on vulnerability as much as the corporate world and its minions, so enjoy being out of that world and able to yell an SOS.

We don't have to be this vision of perfection. Nobody is perfect. No one can connect to that

In her research into vulnerability, Brené Brown found that the interviewees who had a strong sense of connection and wholeheartedness all embraced vulnerability. "They were willing to let go of who they thought they should be, in order to be who they were. You have to absolutely do that for connection. The other thing they had in common was that they fully embraced vulnerability. They believed that what made them vulnerable, made them beautiful."[50]

That first sentence is the real defining point for me and explains exactly the transformation that happened for me in moving from employment to self-employment. When you see the real human – including their strengths AND their flaws – it opens up another way of seeing them, and it is more relatable and beautifully human. We don't have to be this vision of perfection. Nobody is perfect. No one can connect to that. Let the cracks of vulnerability show, and you will find people respond to you in a whole different way.

OVER TO YOU

How do you view others who show vulnerability?

....

....

....

....

....

How comfortable are you with being vulnerable? And
with which kinds of vulnerability (for example, personal,
challenges of running a business, asking for help)?

....

....

....

....

....

....

Is it something you are willing to try? If so, where is the
best place to try?

....

....

....

....

....

....

THE TROLL UNDER THE BRIDGE

If there is one thing I have learnt these last few years, it is that some people make a living out of being offended and/or being a git. My other half calls these people the 'professionally offended'. And you do start to spot them – people that take offence to anything and everything or have an opinion on how everyone should run their business and share their 'advice'. They seem to lurk online purely to feck up your mood for the whole day. To add to the insult, it is often when you least expect it or when you are just having a rare moment of feeling good about something and posted something which you think no one could take any possible offence to. But then the wolf appears at your door, and, of course, when working for yourself, you are the one that is going to have to deal with them.

> *Some people make a living out of being offended and/ or being a git*

So, what's the best way to deal with them? To continue to put yourself out there, and be unapologetically you. If someone doesn't like something you have posted on social media, they can either:

a) Scroll on by, or
b) Bugger off.

(And you may tell them that. I give you permission.)

Unfortunately, many take route c) Be a pompous moron.

Even if you justify yourself, reason with them, apologise, grovel and beg for forgiveness, these oxygen vampires will never see your point of view or accept it. Or occasionally they will see they are losing a battle and vamoose before you can get the last word. So annoying.

It is amazing what people can take offence to, or just be jealous of and therefore give you grief. These bitter creatures are great at making presumptions about you, taking your words out of context or just missing the bloody point. Sometimes I will try to explain, justify or persuade, but generally I have learnt it is just not worth it. These heathens don't budge once they've made their tiny minds up. If the situation warrants, that is what block functions are for. I have developed a five-pronged approach to this.

1. Respond constructively.
2. Kill with kindness.
3. Enlist the troops to help the fight.
4. Block them.
5. Delete the post.

I usually get to stage three or four.

The point of telling you this?

Have a strategy for dealing with it and don't get too caught up in it. You can waste hours and gain a lot of grey hairs with the fallout. But if you must get the last word, as I often do, process the comment(s), rectify (if needed), and move on.

Consider where your boundaries are for what you are willing to put up with and how you may respond so when it happens (because it likely will at some point, as you increase your visibility), you will have something in place to help you decide how to respond.

You may just learn not to give a stuff what the trolls think. I rollercoaster between fight, flight and ignore depending on my mood and levels of stress, overwhelm or fatigue. If nothing else, it will give you social media content for a good week or two.

I have learnt this the hard way (don't mention Gretagate[51]) and I don't generally post anything remotely inflammatory. I can't be bothered and that is not what I am about. But once in a while I will say something, totally unaware of how some random may twist my words or meaning (what a metaphor for the corporate world).

Once you get more confident in just being yourself, it does get easier to deal with and you will learn some good comebacks. I recommend checking out Clair Stevenson[52] and Jo Watson[53] for how they do this, 'cos they don't half attract 'em. But keep in mind it even gets them down sometimes.

> "I do feel I can be myself in business, although it can get me a lot of grief ... I get a lot of trolls. And no, I don't mean people disagreeing with me or being a bit vocal against an opinion of mine they don't value. I mean like people telling me I'm a disgrace of a woman and that I'll burn in hell because I swear. Sigh."
> **Jo**

Leave my Jo alone, you miserable turnips.

OVER TO YOU

Think about how you plan to deal with people that troll or offend you – do you want to react? Or do you have the envious superpower to ignore? Will you kill with kindness? Try to justify your view? Or will you just block and delete?

BUILDING A BARRICADE

Let's turn to the barriers we may face in our businesses. There are two types of barriers – those put up by others, and those you put up yourself.

You may not be able to do much about those Donald Trump-style walls put up by others, though it is sometimes worth a try to make sure your assumptions or beliefs are correct, and to maybe help others to chip away at their walls. But there is damn sure something you can do about the very-quick-to-erect defensive walls we throw up around ourselves.

This was a very telling statement I wrote in a blog post back in 2020: "I had been putting so many barriers up for myself without even realising. Worrying about what certain people think about me, my work, my life. People who matter in no way at all. Why was I still letting them have any control over my life?"[54]

This was followed quickly by the profound insight, "Stop giving a crap what donkeys from your past think". I do amaze myself with my wisdom sometimes.

Anyhoo.

What are some examples of these quick-build walls we put up ourselves?

- The way you tell yourself you can't do something, even if there is no evidence to back that up.
- Caring too much about what others think so you don't pursue what you really want to.
- Telling yourself your family won't be supportive, even though you haven't given them a chance to demonstrate otherwise.
- Letting others impose their self-limiting beliefs onto you.

- Telling yourself you don't have enough experience, aren't thin/pretty/young enough to do that thing you want to do.

Often barriers can come from beliefs others have instilled in us.

An aversion to doing presentations as an ex-boss once told you that you are rubbish at them.

Stop giving a crap what donkeys from your past think

The old school teacher who told you that you would never be able to write because you have dyslexia.

That you will never be a manager as you don't have the right people skills.

Sometimes harmful comments are thrown out in such a flippant manner without any awareness or consideration of the long-term impact they can have. Sometimes it was not even 'meant', you just caught someone at a bad time. Sometimes it can be projection due to their own unfulfilment, or even jealousy. But what these insult flingers don't realise is these things can sink in. We'll then look for other evidence to back up their beliefs and let them fester until they become very real. We don't go for that promotion as we believe we won't get it, or we never write that book because it would surely be a failure (gulp!).

How many times in life have we heard or said "they didn't mean it" or "don't let it get to you"? But it does hurt and it's hard to forget when it's personal.

Particularly when we're younger, vulnerable or inexperienced, we put a lot of stock in what people tell us about ourselves, and it's the negatives that stick with us. I could probably recite from memory a long, long list of all the negative things I have ever been told about myself, yet I have to have my book of wins and a social proof folder to trawl through to remember the good.

It is a weird quirk of our lizard brain that it works this way. We internalise the negatives and let the positives pass by while cringing in embarrassment. (Admit it – I know this is not just me.) In true British awkwardness, we feel we shouldn't share our wins as it would be 'bragging'.

When I went solo, a barrier I created for myself was worrying too much about what other people might think, especially ex-colleagues and employers. Due to the stressed and fractured mental and physical space I inhabited at the time of leaving, I felt embarrassed and wanted to hide away. I felt that others had seen my 'failure'. They had seen me at my worst; they saw me lose that battle. My pride was severely dinted and I was not comfortable with how they last saw me. I let this impact how visible I was initially in setting up the business. I didn't want to inhabit the same space as they did while I was pulling myself back together. But I was still in the same industry and networks, and so I knew I had to face them sooner or later.

We internalise the negatives and let the positives pass by while cringing in embarrassment

I quickly learnt that a benefit of the digital age is that I can show how I am doing so well now, how things have improved and that I have found my fit. I can tell my story of how I have moved on and left the corporate life behind without an ounce of regret. The benefit of hindsight is that I now don't care what they think, apart from a couple of people I am still in touch with, and it is quite nice to be in the position of "Woooooo, look at me now!"

We can sometimes use barriers as an excuse to not move on, to not do something we fear. Because that is what it usually is – fear. Fear of what others may think, fear of things we have no control over, fear of failing or doing wrong. That is what we have been conditioned to do – fear anything negative. But fear holds us back. It stops us achieving long-held dreams.

And no one wants that.

Don't let those donkeys be a barrier ... They're a pain in the ass.

(HA! I made myself laugh at least.)

What barriers do you have relating to your business and working for yourself? Did you create these yourself, or were external factors involved too?

....
....
....
....
....
....
....
....
....
....

How are they stopping you from progressing?

....
....
....
....
....
....
....
....
....
....

BE MORE GEEK

This may come as no surprise given the industry I work in (learning design, in case you missed it), but I am an eternal student. I have always been an avid learner and a restless soul, ever since I was young, when I would take on every arty, sporty and musical extracurricular activity going. This mentality has continued into adulthood, making me a true lifelong learner.

For me, learning never stops. In fact, I constantly try to learn too many new things and need to rein myself in a bit to focus on one or two at a time. I have so many courses in progress I had to create a separate to-do list just for professional development.

I get too giddy. I always have numerous courses, podcasts, fiction and non-fiction books, groups, workshops and how-to guides on the go at any one time, both for things I am learning in my industry and the business and also for my hobbies. It is surprising where some of the random skills I have learnt over the years come in too, when I can dredge them from the recesses of my memory.

What's so good about learning?

For a start, I truly believe it does wonders for your mental health.

Learning can be great for our brains. It gives a sense of growth, fulfilment, intrigue and experimentation. It gives us a dopamine hit with every successful outcome, no matter how small.

It uses creativity and encourages self-care. It can encourage interaction with others in shared interest groups, and the sharing of skills. It develops transferable skills. If you want to get scientific about it, continual learning into late adulthood has also been shown to help stave off conditions such as dementia.[55]

There is something magical about the feeling of being immersed in a new topic or skill – exploring and testing the waters to see what happens or learning about a topic from a new perspective. It keeps the mind occupied and away from anything that may stress the mind instead.

Then there is also the joyous feeling of accomplishment that comes with mastering something, even just a small part of an overall task (such as remembering a word in a new language or finally nailing a step in a new process). A momentary firing of serotonin and endorphins that makes you feel great, powerful, ready to conquer the world. Or one teeny tiny part of it at least.

Being able to share the knowledge learnt to help others is great too – this was the part of lecturing that I loved (unfortunately everything else that came with that job overshadowed this). A lot of the crochet I do is for others – either for charities or gifts. I enjoy being able to create something that others can benefit from or enjoy.

Most importantly – continual learning keeps me busy. I have always been quite (hmm, extremely) restless and struggle to rest as much as I should. I am not someone that can just sit and watch TV for hours, or even sit through a film. I feel the need to be doing something. Crochet and reading are great for this as I have to sit to do them. They are the only things that make me able to just vegetate, recoup and listen to some mindless

Learning gives us a dopamine hit with every successful outcome, no matter how small

Netflix programme in the background (or whatever is my latest music obsession on a never-ending loop), but feel productive at the same time. Spending half an hour learning something new instead of watching depressing, mindless drivel like Eastenders is a much better use of my time, and much better for the brain.

It is no coincidence how often someone will comment to me that they don't have time to read, yet in the next breath ask me if I watched X, Y and Z last night. I don't feel like it is a case of finding the time. I want to do it and so these things become a natural part of my day.

And if something goes wrong in the process of learning, that is okay. We've all been there, we all started at the beginning. It is not a place of judgement. You never know, you could actually have a happy accident – I love those moments when something magical happens and you can claim "yeah, that's what I planned to happen" when that actually couldn't be further from the truth.

When I was teaching, I spent so much time trying to wrestle the teenagers from the paralysing fear of something not working to just try and experiment. At that age, the fear of messing something up in front of their peers and making something non-Instagram-worthy is indeed too big a risk for many. As we get older, that fear vanishes. But if your head is in a bad place, you may find it resurfaces, particularly if you have been in a work environment where you suffered a lot of criticism and unwarranted feedback.

The downside of this continual inquisitive nature is that I have become a master of taking on too many things. I want to learn everything. I rarely finish one thing before I start three more, and this can actually lead to quite a bit of stress and cognitive overload. Plus, the lack of finishing much means that you never get to experience that lovely dopamine that comes with completing something and having a tangible product or skill that you can show off.

Being surrounded by numerous half-done projects across many types of craft can be a continual reminder of how much I have to do. (It also appears to greatly annoy my other half.) Some of the learning inevitably vamooses into thin air and gets forgotten due to competing for memory space and not being practised frequently enough. And occasionally, just as I've got going, the need to learn something goes away due to a change in jobs. Frustrating, much?

The more you can focus on what you need NOW, the better. Try not to sign up to things with the aim that you will get to 'one day'. Your priorities may have changed by the time you have space in your schedule to do it. Then you must deal with the inevitable frustration of having wasted time and money, and having had the extra task looming on your to-do list for way too long. If, like me, you love to tick things off the list, this can be quite the ongoing pain.

If you need any more convincing, in *Company of One*, Paul Jarvis tells how he was the geek that everyone picked on in school and how he had to hide his personality as a result. Years later, in trying to understand why people were buying from his business, he surveyed his customers to find out – and there was an overwhelmingly common response.

> "What changed? My personality didn't. I'm still an awkward and excitable nerd, just like I was in high school. What did change was that I gradually became okay with sharing who I am and using my differences strategically. Once who I am became part of how I marketed and sold, more people started to respond to that... They trusted me because of my personality, since a lot of them were awkward and excitable nerds too."[56]

Geeks for the win. It had to be our day, one day.

OVER TO YOU

Write a list of at least three things/topics/skills you would like to learn, either for business or pleasure. Maybe they are something you have wanted to learn for a while but not got around to starting.

....

....

....

....

....

Take some time to look into some great resources and put a plan together for how you are going to learn.

....

....

....

....

....

Will it be daily through an app (and can you set a reminder so you do it)?

....

....

....

....

....

....

Will you set aside a weekly time to focus solely on it?

....

....

....

....

....

....

Will you join a network or community to learn?

....

....

....

....

....

....

Which would be most beneficial for you right now?

....

....

....

....

....

....

ON RECHARGE

Balance. Self-care. Recharge. Rest. Recovery.

I know what I SHOULD do, but do I do it…?

These are some of the hardest things for me to achieve in business and life. They are always just out of reach as I prioritise everything except myself. I take on too much and get giddy. Start a gazillion new projects before I have finished the last dozen.

It is a continual learning process for me to make sure I schedule projects well, make myself take time out and eat healthily. As much as I class many of my side projects as a form of self-care because I enjoy doing them, I know I am kidding myself and that I need to make time for proper physical and mental rest.

Working from home, I find it so hard to down tools when there is always more that can be done, or another task to tick off. It is too easy to take the laptop downstairs with me or to start responding to email on my phone at all hours. I sign up to loads of webinars that take place in the evening or at lunch. Replace 'entrepreneurs' with something else, and this statement sums me up perfectly:

> "Entrepreneurs are the only people who will work 80 hours a week to avoid working 40 hours a week for someone else."
> **Lori Greiner**[57]

I have enjoyed working for myself so much that I haven't (yet) minded working crazy hours, but it is not sustainable long term. I have had to start holding myself accountable to self-care. For me, that takes the shape of a stupidly expensive gym membership, to guilt me into getting out and exercising. Promising myself I will go for a (free) walk every day just doesn't happen – there is nothing to hold me accountable to that. Unless someone comes and calls for me every day to walk me like a pet dog, I have no chance. Other priorities take over. It is always 'I'll do it tomorrow'.

During the pandemic suddenly everyone was going for daily walks and bike rides, running and taking up a range of active hobbies to get outside. I started to feel so guilty that I was doing none of this and realised that was where I was significantly lacking in looking after myself. As I was one of the lucky ones whose business boomed in this time, I went the other way – I chained myself to my desk working silly hours (then also decided to write a book. Ha!). When I got to the point that I realised I hadn't had a day off in two years except for two days at Christmas, I realised things needed to change.

"As a self-employed freelancer you have to look after yourself, 'cos no one else will" – Giles

I started booking into yoga sessions that you cannot cancel in the 24 hours before so I couldn't escape doing them. When the world opened up again, I took myself off to my two favourite bookstores and bought a supply of books I had been wanting for a while, as a treat to make myself sit and read. And I booked time in my diary for all this so I couldn't double-book myself or feel guilty at taking that time out. If anything, my colour-coded Google diary showed me how little time I took for myself. I realised I needed to step back, switch off and enlist more support from my VA. I am getting there, little by little.

Giles has self-care much more sussed, recognising when he needs to take time out to recharge his batteries and acknowledging the mindset adjustment it has taken, having come from an always-on, work hard play hard corporate culture in Leeds. He advises that you need to make time – and take time – to look after your own mental health and well-being so that you can keep all your plates spinning.

> "Pushing yourself until you drop, or being pushed by the corporate machinery of your employer until you're burnt-out and have a nervous breakdown, isn't a badge of honour or something to be proud of. It's negative and harmful. As a self-employed freelancer you have to look after yourself, 'cos no one else will."

Crikey, good point. Consider myself told.

There is a point where you realise, if you make yourself ill, then no one is there to do the work instead. And you don't want to wait until you are burnt out to realise this.

One of the best ways I have learnt to increase self-care is to learn to say NO – to things I don't want to do, have no time for, are against my principles, below the rate I accept, or would require skills I just don't have.

> "It's about finding a new way of doing business: one that works for your bank account and supports your well-being; one that works for you and the planet; and one that follows the path of least resistance."
> **Denise Duffield-Thomas, *Chillpreneur*[58]**

What does self-care look like for you?

....
....
....
....
....

How can you make sure you make time to recharge?

....
....
....
....
....

How will you hold yourself accountable to it?

....
....
....
....
....

JUST. NO.

> "In their eagerness to please, [some freelancers] end up taking on too much, letting people down and ultimately just burning themselves out. Saying no is vital to safeguard your business, the quality of your service and, ultimately, your own well-being."
> **Tom Albrighton, *The Freelance Introvert*** [59]

One of the most important skills you will learn in self-employment is to say no, ranging in scale from "Hell no!" to a polite "No. Sorry, I cannot fit that in right now. Please, I beg forgiveness."

In the early years, in particular, there is a temptation to take anything and everything on, and then it is hard to let this go. You can feel like you should never say no. That if you do, then a dry spell will hit and you will regret it. However, you need to find the balance and trust your instincts. If you do not learn this skill, a few things can happen (and I speak from experience here).

- You end up working on projects that you knew were going to be a pain, or that you wouldn't enjoy. And they prove you right.
- You end up burnt out from taking too much on.
- You get paid less than you wanted when the inevitable bartering from a customer worked to their advantage as you didn't feel confident enough to stand your ground.
- You spread yourself too thin (and I write this while spread so nano-thin).
- You don't end up with much time for family, hobbies and self-care.
- You end up doing things or giving your time away for free to those "can I just pick your brain for 10 minutes?" types. It is never just 10 minutes. My brain has been picked so many times it is no wonder there only appear to be crumbs of it left.

Saying no is a heck of a challenge and I am guilty of every one of those points in the list above. The challenge in saying no comes back to those boundaries that you need to set for yourself and that I love bashing down so eagerly. Now I am aware of it, I am working on it. It happens less frequently, and the bartering from clients doesn't go as low as I used to let it. I have developed something of an internal monologue which lets me know when I am skirting a bit too close to a yes and shouldn't be.

It has been a long, hard road for me to get to the point where I finally realise the type of projects I want to pursue, the type of clients I want, and to have the guts to say I am not interested in others. Unfortunately, there is not a magic switch you can just flip, so you cannot always guarantee a project will turn out as marvellous as it looks in the scoping stages. Any number of complications could kick in and you may still end up with one that is a pain in the arse. But at least you can reduce the potential for pain by being selective in the projects you take on, weeding out some of the bad ones and those you know you won't enjoy.

My journey to NO

I am a perpetual people pleaser and so hate to turn people down. Plus, I get so excited about everything, and want to do ALL THE THINGS. So, I take on all the things. Then regret it, as even with the best scheduling that could be achieved, inevitable delays mean clashing projects and deadlines, and continual double/triple booking of meetings. I end up knackered, swearing I will never get in this position again. But I do learn something each time. I think.

Quite early on in self-employment I started to feel like a pushover as I was saying yes when I didn't want to, and that was not having a great impact on my mind. In employment I had learnt that I was to be silenced, and was not to stand up for myself. So I carried this into self-employment at first, before I realised what I was doing and dug my confidence out of the pit in which it sat. Some of the pushover feelings were exacerbated when I started to really resent some low-paid projects I was working on (a hangover of clients from when I first started freelancing on the side), or the client wasn't particularly nice to me. (One plonker regularly made condescending remarks about women and designers, so why he kept coming back to me I'll never know.) This is not the best or most efficient way to work. But this is where I found myself.

I am pretty drunk on the power those two little letters give when used correctly

So, I started to say no.

And it is pretty addictive.

I am pretty drunk on the power those two little letters give when used correctly.

The power of no-drunkenness is joyous. It is a revelation.

I had never realised how good it is for your mental health to have and use such a small word as no. And even better – nothing bad has come from saying no. Though they may be disappointed, clients respect you for being honest and saying you are too busy, and couldn't give the job the time it requires to do a bloody good job. They are quite often further intrigued to work with me as they see a calendar that is full for the next six months as a reflection of my work.

One of the best ways to find your no power is to make sure you are aware of why you want to say no. Is it because you don't want to do something, because you can't do something, or is it something you shouldn't do? These are three very different motivations behind your answer. By being aware of them, they can help you decide whether you would be open to bartering, or future opportunities if the situation allowed.

As business owners, I think we have all had times, especially in the early days, where we have said yes to some work, knowing full well we didn't want to but for the sake of eating more than beans and rice that month we've had to. But once you are past that position, if you really don't want to do something, and you are comfortable enough with the work you have on and have money coming in, then unleash the no power.

> "It's your right to live on your own terms... it's okay to say no whenever you goddamn please, to whomever you goddamn must, and you don't have to be so goddamn sorry about it."
> **Sarah Knight, *F**k No!*[60]**

How can you make it easier to say no?

1. Have a pool of people you can happily refer potential clients on to if you are too busy to fit them in. The client will be very appreciative of this, and will remember you very favourably as a result.

2. If you feel you need to, explain why you are saying no. You absolutely do not have to explain to anyone, but if, like me, you feel bad or awkward, then briefly say why it is a no, especially if it is a customer you would like to come back at some point. Try this sentence: "I would love to but I just can't fit it into my schedule right now. Would you like me to give you details of other freelancers who may be able to help you?"

    If you don't give a stuff, don't bother.

3. Don't skirt around the subject. Just be clear and come out with it – if you don't want to do it, tell them you are not the best fit for the project, it doesn't fit with your interests, or whatever reason you have. If you fib and say it was due to time or money, they might come back to pester more or start

bartering and you'll end up unable to get rid of them. They need a straight answer, and you need to make it clear this is not time for negotiation.

4. Consider your motivation for saying no. If the project is against your principles, or something you really just don't want to do, then say no and move on.

5. Remember that in saying no to things you don't want to do, you are making way for more fabulous projects to come through. There are a few times I have been gutted that I have accepted a project I wasn't fussed about, then something amazing popped up instead that I couldn't do as a result.

6. Have a stock set of phrases ready to use for differing occasions.

I highly recommend Sarah Knight's book *F**k No!* if this is something you particularly need to work on. She provides suggestions for reframing queries, saying no in a manner of guises and has a helpful flow chart[61] to help you decide if you should say yes or no.

You could be forgiven for ignoring anything I have said and just heading to the flowchart and letting it rule your life and decisions.

Next time you want to, Just Say No.

(I so hope all of you above a certain age are now singing the dreaded song.)

What do you find most difficult to say no to? And why?
(Remember the don't want to/can't/shouldn't.)

....
....
....
....
....
....

What difficulties has this caused for you in the past?

....
....
....
....
....
....

What steps can you put in place to join me in getting drunk
on the power of no?

....
....
....
....
....
....
....

AIM FOR GOOD

> "Have no fear of perfection. You'll never reach it."
> **Salvador Dali**

So often we think in black and white. Everything is 'shit' or everything is 'perfect'. We see the perfection in others but not ourselves. We can let perfectionism stop us doing things we really want to do, or let it tell us that we are not good enough.

But is perfection even achievable?

Surely by its own definition, there will always be something that could be improved. As a result, it can paralyse any further action, or even getting started. Perfectionism views the end goal as more important than the process or the learning that can take place. It suggests there is no subjectivity for each person's definition of what the perfect outcome is. It leads to unhealthy fears of retribution as perfection is not achieved. It leads to jealously of others' successes.

We rarely see ourselves as perfect and tend to veer the other way, believing ourselves to be inadequate. In her marvellous Freelance Heroes Day 2020 talk on perfectionism,[62] Honor Clement-Hayes proposed that we should "aim for good". That is a much less stressful and more joyful place to be. And sometimes "good enough is good enough".

Perfectionism views the end goal as more important than the process

She's right, you know.

From a young age, we are conditioned to think in perfect terms and that winning is everything. Through school, we are taught that a hundred per cent is the end goal of every exam or assessment. We must ace driving tests, presentations, academic exams, and meet endless (moving) goalposts. We have to pass probationary periods in jobs, when we already succeeded at interview, then have annual appraisals where we must achieve top scores to have any hope of progression. We should always finish what we started – not abandon anything part way through, lest we show ourselves to be lacking commitment and perseverance.

To put it bluntly, there is no room for even a little error, never mind more major catastrophes, so we live in fear of ever making the slightest mistake or error in judgement.

Often the perfection we are trying to achieve is a fabrication of our own minds, and not what the client was necessarily expecting, or at times is even grateful for. More often than not, they certainly haven't paid for perfection. It is the result of comparing ourselves unfavourably to others.

WE'RE GOING TO RELENTLESSLY CHASE PERFECTION, KNOWING FULL WELL WE WILL NOT CATCH IT... IN THE PROCESS WE WILL CATCH EXCELLENCE.

VINCE LOMBARDI, QUOTED BY ERIK KESSELS IN
FAILED IT! [63]

Now *that* is how to look at it. We need to learn when to say it's good enough and not strive for something that was unattainable anyway.

I like Denise Duffield-Thomas's perspective on this topic, who says that we don't have to be revolutionary, and we don't have to be saying something never heard before. We just have to be telling a story from our perspective to the people who need to hear it. Sure, there are people who may react negatively – but they are not the ones who needed to hear it. When you find those people who do, you have hit gold. This statement alone has changed my perception of a few things.

> "I became a lot less precious about my work because I knew it didn't have to be completely groundbreaking or unique to make a difference to the people who needed to hear it from me."
> **Denise Duffield-Thomas, *Chillpreneur*[64]**

You should also aim for wrong. In the next section, we'll look at why.

OVER TO YOU

Reflect on where perfectionism stops you in your tracks. Where is the level where you can say it is good enough?

....

....

....

....

....

Where do your perceptions of perfect come from in relation to your business?

....

....

....

....

....

WONDERFULLY WRONG

> "Success is the ability to go from failure to failure without losing your enthusiasm."
> **Winston Churchill**

Mistakes and failures – they will happen. And it is a good thing when they do.

Honestly.

Even big businesses make them. And large or small, they may hurt the same.

Mistakes and failures are part of the creative process. They show you are experimenting, trying new avenues, and pushing yourself. Playwright Samuel Beckett famously said, "Ever tried. Ever failed. No matter. Try again. Fail again. Fail better." I really resonate with the idea of failing better and taking steps towards something great. When I look back at my previous experiences in employment, I now try to look at it this way. I may feel like I have had a series of failures, but I have learnt something with each one, and they have led me to something amazing – self-employment. Each failed attempt at employment gave me a different set of experiences that have led to me now being able to offer a unique set of skills to my clients.

And I still make mistakes or have failures every week, but they bother me a lot less now. It might be a contract I didn't win, or a client who moves on to another provider. An error I spotted after I had sent the files to the client. A talk that didn't go amazingly well. But there will be a reason why it has happened, and it is not necessarily even to do with me; maybe someone else was just a better fit for a project, or had better experience in a certain industry. The tech caused huge problems and fecked up your online talk. I have even launched a product which I would class as a failure.

It is how you deal with mistakes that is the defining factor, and will say more about you than the brag of another win. Social media is full of seemingly perfect people – with businesses booming, perfectly coiffed hair on all calls, winning awards … but a lot of these people are afraid to show their mistakes. To show their imperfections. To have a laugh at their own expense. And I am all about that.

"Ever tried.
Ever failed.
No matter.
Try again.
Fail again.
Fail better" –
Samuel Beckett

I have found that the social media content where I expose my mistakes and difficulties are those that get most engagement. Those where I make fun of my 'blondeness' and clumsiness garner the banter. These posts resonate with people; they stand out among the seeming perfection. Content can be found in everything, and the more disaster-led it is, the more people relate. Serial entrepreneur Denise Duffield-Thomas has made many mistakes and had failure on her path to success. She says of it, "Everything is useful, and nothing is wasted. In fact, failures are great fodder for podcasts, blog posts, and future Oprah interviews."[65]

Dealing with it

Often, you cannot prepare for mistakes and failures. The very nature of them is unexpected. If we saw them coming, they wouldn't happen, right? And to sit waiting for them is not a nice way to live. But you *can* have a process for dealing with them.

If there is one thing I have learnt from dealing with cowboy builders on our new-build house – admit your mistakes, apologise and rectify it. That is all we ask. Don't try to hide it, don't paper over the (literal) cracks and when you say you're going to fix it, turn up and damn well fix it. This seems like basic customer service, but apparently it isn't for some companies.

It's hard to admit to mistakes, and you may not have to if it doesn't really involve anyone else. But if it does, you can apologise and promptly resolve it, and it will soon be forgotten. It will only be you ruminating on it at 3am (there's a habit to stop...).

Advertising executive Sir John Hegarty suggests a different approach: "Many people talk about failures as opportunities to learn. Saying this seems to make people feel wise and worldly. Well, I say bollocks to failure. Don't dwell on it. Move on. Forget it."[66]

If only it was that easy, eh?

Despite what he says, and as clichéd as it is to say it, I think we do learn from our mistakes. I have learnt many a thing about the type of projects I enjoy working on, after taking on some nightmare. I have undercharged and missed opportunities to increase my rates in a moment of confidence crisis. I know where my skills lie after trying new things that I just couldn't get a handle on. And I have posted things that I later wished I hadn't, therefore learning the boundaries of things I should share. If you are open to some trial and error, which I highly recommend, you can have fun, as you test things out, break the mould or cock up magnificently and share the disaster with your world.

You can have fun, as you test things out, break the mould or cock up magnificently and share the disaster with your world

A big change for me came when I started to think about the language I was using and the way my self-talk influenced my emotions. This has a huge influence on how you interpret things.

At my lowest ebb I was continually berating myself over mistakes (including things that were out of my control). I was using words like 'failure', 'messed up', 'fucked up' on an hourly basis. I continually exclaimed, "I don't know why I bother." These words were often stronger than the situation warranted, but it didn't feel like that at the time.

We had an interesting chat about this in a recent business book club, where someone mentioned they used software for tracking potential leads, and it asked you to mark them as 'won' or 'lost'. Quite rightly, she didn't like that as it wasn't necessarily about winning or losing. It's not that black and white. Sometimes, there is someone else better suited to that project. Maybe it fell outside of your niche. Maybe you couldn't fit it into your packed schedule. These are not failures or missed opportunities. These are sensible decisions, to say, "Thank you for the opportunity but I think (this person) would be better suited" or "I can't do it right now. My next available slot is…" A reframe is needed. It was an opportunity, it didn't work out, but it is creating room for a better one.

The debate here isn't about how to stop yourself making mistakes. I actively encourage you to make them. If you don't make mistakes, if you don't fail, it means you haven't experimented, or pushed yourself, or attempted to learn anything new. I'm glad to say Sarah Townsend agrees. "I hope that in this year to come, you make mistakes. Because if you are making mistakes, then you are making new things, trying new things, learning, living, pushing yourself, changing the world."[67]

Plus, you never know when a happy accident is just around the corner.

> "Perhaps the mistakes and circumstances that join forces to create failure are not your mortal enemy but are, in fact, the key elements in producing something new and exciting."
> **Erik Kessels,** *Failed It!*[68]

255

Think of a recent event where you felt like you failed or made a mistake. How can you reframe this? What were the factors involved that led to it?

....

....

....

....

....

....

If required, how did you rectify it?

....

....

....

....

....

Did you move on quickly afterwards? Or did you ruminate on it for an age? How do you feel about it now?

....

....

....

....

....

....

THE HARDEST WORD TO SAY

"Help!"

One of the hardest words to say, yet one of the best words you can say. A word which can round up an army. A word which can answer a question you have been pondering over for hours. Days even. A little word with huge power.

So, why don't we say it?

Because we worry it'll look like we don't know what we're doing. We worry what others may think. Worry that it will make us look weak. Or stupid. We worry who will see our post. And what the response might be. And, yes, there are occasionally arsey, condescending responses or trolls, but they are few and far between if you are in the right communities.

One of the hardest words to say, yet one of the best

As I mentioned earlier, as a business owner, we have to do lots of things out of our comfort zone. We have to do accounts, run a website, put marketing campaigns together, pitch work, manage our sales ... but we cannot know everything. There is a world of business owners out there with tried and tested solutions to all our problems, so don't hold back. There really is no stupid question.

Whether your problem is:

- A crisis of confidence.
- Not having a clue where to start with web hosting.
- A customer being a total pain in the arse and messing you about (or not paying!).
- Being unexpectedly charged by HMRC for the mystery that is payment on account.

- Having stared at something too long and lost all sense of perspective, and need some input as to whether A or B is better.
- Just needing a place to rant and share hate for the never-ending trial that is WordPress.
- Or any other myriad of things that we just want human input on.

I have asked (mmm, ranted) questions about all of these in online communities and not one person has been a dick about it. And this doesn't even touch the surface of the stupid things I ask my accountant. When others responded to share their experiences and advice, I felt validated, not stupid. I felt seen. I received answers, solutions, virtual hugs. I have even accidentally enlisted some to help me with a very persistent troll.

As well as the responses, it cannot be underestimated how much time it can save you to just ask for help; how a different perspective can help you make that decision you have been mulling over for hours or even days. You'll feel so much more powerful with a tribe of freelancers who have your back.

Recently, I asked the relatively simple question of what website building platform people recommended for my book website – that wasn't WordPress, 'cos me and it are obviously not friends. I had already researched the options, and knew the prices, but I wanted to see how others had experienced the platforms. I wanted to know what they thought about the building process (for someone with few web skills). And I got more than that

You'll feel so much more powerful with a tribe of freelancers who have your back

back – I found out about the companies' customer service, the reliability of the platforms, the ease with which a website could be produced and the speed at which you could get it up and running. Things that you cannot get from just looking at what the companies say. It is valued input which helped me to make my decision. Help that I could not have researched on my own. (And they were right: Squarespace is marvellous.)

The more you help others out with their questions, the more you will build relationships and a community. And the more responses you will get when it is time to ask for help yourself.

As Joelle can testify, "The answer to anything this life throws at you is out there if you look. Find the right people to walk alongside you, design your business around the life you want to live and believe in your abilities. And if you need a little help, just like I did, there is absolutely no shame in getting it. If nothing else, I'm proof that there is a happily ever after."

OVER TO YOU

Take a look in the communities you are a part of and see
where you could provide your musings or experiences on
a question asked.

....

....

....

....

....

....

Are there particular topics you think you could help others
with? Where might those types of questions appear? Make
a plan to go and join in the conversation.

....

....

....

....

....

....

Identify some burning questions of your own. Which
community is the best place to ask for input?

....

....

....

....

....

....

CRAWLING OUT FROM
UNDER MY ROCK

Getting comfortable with standing out can be one of the more challenging aspects of promoting yourself if you are not confident. Especially if your confidence has taken a battering in your previous roles. You need to spend time finding your way of doing it.

You will find a whole raft of techniques used by others and as tempting as it can be to imitate them, you will not get far in copying others. The lack of genuineness will be clear, and someone is likely to call you out on it.

You only need to take a quick scroll on LinkedIn to see how some have endless wit and sarcasm, others swear, some are brutally open and honest, or go in for countless awards. Others have hidden more of themselves to purely focus on showing their industry knowledge or practical skills, through articles, resources and helpful blog posts. Some people stand out because they are doing good in the world – they talk about their values, they show the value they can offer. Or they may just be bloody lovely people, ridiculously helpful, and their clients may even do the shouting out for them.

You don't have to be confident, controversial, arrogant or shout loudly to stand out

You don't have to be confident, controversial, arrogant or shout loudly to stand out. Here are some examples of freelancers who really stand out on their own and how they do it, with not a flutter of controversy or being the loudest freelancer on the block.

First up, Alice Hollis.[69] She has a ridiculously helpful and informative blog, plus regularly produces 'Little Books' which she gives away for free (!). When I requested the print version, they arrived branded in a shiny purple envelope (her brand colour, which is prevalent throughout her business) with other little treats. She manages to do all of this while being a lovely, down-to-earth and authentic person, who genuinely wants to help. Not an ounce of arrogance or brashness in sight. Just loveliness and knowledge.

Dee Primett of Wicked Creative[70] is another that stands out. I am in a few communities with Dee and she is ALWAYS there to help others when they ask questions, have a bad day, to celebrate your victories with you, and to be the friend you never knew you had. She gives knowledgeable, balanced advice and has now also set up the Female Copywriters Alliance to help big up the ladies, as well as always bigging up the FFC (the Fabulous Freelance Community), as she calls it. An activist all of our own. Lovely stuff.

Then you have Ellen and Craig Boyle, the duo behind Content By The Sea.[71] They are making great strides not just in their professional work but by opening up the conversation around mental health and breaking down some of the ever-present stigma. The newsletter gets a great response every Wednesday morning and the fairly recent addition of the Conversations By The Sea podcast is a fabulous, open conversation on the combination of mental health and running a business.

And there is fellow Yorkshire-based Penny Brazier of The Mighty Pen.[72] This is a lady whose writing, style, humour, persona, general music knowledge and genius I am in awe of. I defo fan-girl Penny. Anyone that can get "Well, blow up my bloomers and stick a quill up my arse" into a sentence about Shakespeare and creativity in lockdown[73], or be revered for an article about David Bowie's bulge[74] is well-deserving of this awe in my opinion. But that aside, she also offers fantastic courses and workshops helping you to find your voice and reach your audience. I still "bathe in my genius" to this day thanks to Penny's advice. In fact, I shall do that right now.

We cannot have such a list without mentioning more about one of the book's stars, the queen of self-employment that is Sophie Cross. But where do we even start? Sophie had a rough start to the pandemic as her specialism of working in the travel and hospitality industry disappeared overnight. But she quickly adapted her business offering to create and sell courses, which received amazing feedback. If that wasn't enough, she pulled it out of the bag by deciding to create *Freelancer Magazine* (see the resources section for a link). After smashing her Kickstarter goals, she launched the magazine, which celebrates freelancers, the freelance life and is quickly establishing a community all of its own. But the thing about Sophie is she is so humble, genuine, and honestly seems disbelieving of her own success. She has built up an army of dedicated followers who appreciate her for just being herself and is now regularly appearing everywhere.[75]

So, we can see the ladies (and Craig) are rocking it. Let's look at what some of the men are doing too.

We can't talk about standing out in the freelance world without mentioning the Big Chiefs that are Steve Folland and Ed Goodman. They run the communities Being Freelance and Freelance Heroes, respectively. These are not just Facebook communities either; there are podcasts, book clubs, awards, conference days, masterminds, Twitter chats, portals, quiz nights ... honestly the list just goes on. Not only are they both providing this fabulous platform (and let's face it, a place for us to get our freelance therapy), they each bring their own brand of wit, humour, warmth and support. You only have to watch the NEOTW (Non-Employee Of The Week) awards and see Steve running around his car park of dreams to realise you have found your place in the world. They have created genuinely lovely places to be, which certainly help freelancers feel less alone. Even my mum has become Ed's biggest fan.

As you can see from these examples, there are two factors at play here – the actual physical offering you give, which provides the value (a resource, a podcast, a community), and the way in which you do it (with personality, authenticity, being helpful). I know I sound a bit gushy and starry-eyed but I adore the freelance community and there are honestly so many people I could have included here, probably a whole book's worth in itself. For now, don't forget to check out the Stars section and the blog at fallingofftheladder.com for more marvellous people and inspirational stories.

When I first launched my business, I took a very practical approach to posting free resources, answering common potential client questions and focusing heavily on industry. That was okay, and it built up a bank of resources, but the big change occurred when I started doing it with more personality and started to feel more confident being myself. My visibility soared, and the algorithm more regularly picked me up due to the better response rates to my content. People started to increasingly comment and engage with the posts, and I was generating more inbound enquiries, particularly on LinkedIn.

Take a look at how you currently promote yourself and answer the following questions.

- Are you providing an object or information of value to your audience?
- Are you infusing it with your personality?
- How can you make it feel even more you?
- And how does it communicate your personal and business values that you defined earlier on in this section?
- What could you do to take it to the next level and stand out from others who offer similar?

Don't be afraid to stand out and stand proud.

OVER TO YOU

Look at the promotions and profiles of other self-employed people, and ask yourself what makes them stand out – is it their offering, tone of voice, use of media, or something else? Could you take any tips from them that suit your personality and approach to build your confidence in putting yourself out there?

....

....

....

....

....

....

Answer the questions above and come up with two things you would like to improve or create from scratch that would offer value and bring in your personality. Now go and do it (and tag me – I want to see your journey).

....

....

....

....

....

....

"

I HAPPEN TO LIKE CHOICES.
I LIKE THAT I CAN CHOOSE
TO MAKE LESS MONEY BY
SAYING NO TO A PROJECT
OR A CLIENT OR A CUSTOMER
I DON'T THINK IS A GOOD
FIT FOR ME. I LIKE THAT I
CAN CHOOSE TO UNPLUG FOR
THREE MONTHS AT A TIME
AND GO ON CAMPING ROAD
TRIPS ACROSS AMERICAN
DESERTS WITH MY WIFE. I
LIKE THAT I CAN PICK WHAT I
WORK ON NEXT, RATHER THAN
HAVE WORK HANDED DOWN TO
ME. I LIKE THAT I CAN WORK
ON SATURDAY IF I WANT, AND
GO HIKING ON WEDNESDAY...
YES, IT'S TAKEN SOME TIME
TO GET HERE, AND I HAD TO

BE OKAY WITH NOT HAVING NEARLY AS MUCH FREEDOM IN THE BEGINNING AS I DO NOW. AFTER ALL, BILLS NEED TO BE PAID AND SOMETIMES THE BEST CLIENT ISN'T THE BEST FIT BUT HE'S THE ONE WHO'S HERE RIGHT NOW AND WILLING TO PAY YOU THIS MONTH. STILL, EVEN IN THE ROUGH PATCHES, MY PURPOSE - MY FREEDOM OF CHOICE - IS WHAT'S DRIVEN ME FORWARD.

PAUL JARVIS, *COMPANY OF ONE*[76]

TOP TIPS FROM THE CONTRIBUTORS

I asked all the contributors in the book,

> **What would be the best piece of advice you would give to someone new to self-employment or about to embark upon it?**

Here are their answers.

Matthew

Give yourself three years to make it profitable. Keep showing up and getting your name out there. Blog loads and post loads of helpful stuff, as well as personal stories, on social media.

But give it three years. Going in with the mindset that you will be making a good living within six months will lead to you failing. If you don't, great, but to get you through the tough days and weeks when work is slow, remember, three years is the magic number.

Joelle

Being self-employed with a business model that includes passive, scalable and automated income streams means that there is NO income ceiling to be squashed against. It's your choice what you earn, how you earn it and how you work with your customers.

The answer to anything this life throws at you is out there if you look. Find the right people to walk alongside you, design your business around the life you want to live and believe in your abilities. And if you need a little help, just like I did, there is absolutely no shame in getting it. If nothing else, I'm proof that there is a happily ever after.

Sophie

Get yourself a support network of other freelancers whether that be on social media, through attending events or joinZ an online community. You have to know you're not going it alone. Everyone has the same problems and freelancers are so supportive. You will learn so much.

Kate

Trust your gut. Accept that you can't do this alone – you don't need people to do the work for you but having others to bounce ideas off and chat about issues you are trying to overcome, even if completely unrelated to your own business, is absolutely essential.

Giles

Don't try and do it alone, or go it alone. No man – nor woman – is an island. You need good people around you, whether that's an accountant, a VA, networking contacts and connections, or a community of like-minded people, such as Freelance Heroes or the Federation of Small Businesses (FSB). Find your tribe – online, on social media and LinkedIn, if not in real life, offline. Networking and working part time out of a co-working space were both massive boosts to me as an individual and to my business too. Having people to talk to helps in every situation, without a doubt. There will be people who will listen, understand and be able to give you advice and support – either personal or professional. There is a great freelance community out there, and it's not hard to find and join in with.

In terms of practical advice, I left it very late to get an accountant and FreeAgent for my invoicing and accounting (other electronic accounting packages are available of course). When you start out, you probably don't have a lot of money to throw around, so an accountant and accounting package might seem like a luxury, but not having them is a false economy. They will pay for themselves in time and effort saved – and in the case of an accountant, money saved on your tax bill, in no time.

Jo

Ignore all the 'six-figure' bollocks on social media. It is precisely that. Bollocks.

Francesca

Well, it honestly depends on what you're after. It's not a dream. But if you thrive off flexibility and variety, why not?

Craig

Check that there is a market for what you do and that it's not over-saturated. Also think about less risky routes into self-employment, such as contracting through an agency first, then going freelance.

Make connections with other freelancers and contractors, even if you initially see them as rivals. There are many helpful people out there with too much work on, and they could pass some your way.

Be kind. Be polite. Be helpful. Respect people's time. Work hard.

Pavitra

Be open to experimenting and manage your income well. Freelancers typically have erratic incomes, and sound financial planning is required to avoid compromising by taking up suboptimal projects due to money crunch. Your time is precious, so make sure you are not spending it on work you don't enjoy. During dry spells, invest your time in continual professional development. This will ensure you keep yourself updated with the latest trends of your industry and rid you of the anxiety that comes with having no projects at hand.

THIS IS ME!

> "I will never promise to be this way or that way, I will only promise to show up, as I am, wherever I am. That's it, and that's all. People will like me or not, but being liked is not my One Thing; integrity is. So I must live and tell my truth."
> **Glennon Doyle, *Untamed*[77]**

Ultimately, the goal is for you to have a thriving business, where you are happy and content, working on projects that you find interesting and which light a fire in you, working with people you connect with, and to be excited (or at least content) in your work.

We spend such a huge amount of our lives working, so you absolutely have the right to feel fulfilled in your work and enjoy what you do. In fact, many of the current working generation may face having to work into their 80s (do NOT get me started on this).

You deserve happiness, to be treated well. You deserve to live life on your own terms

As we come to the end of the book (sniff), your challenge is to combine everything, to put it into practice, to put yourself out there. And to go full throttle – unleash the full you, the real you, the you that actually feels like you. Build on the confidence and self-belief that you are starting to develop and the story you are rediscovering about yourself. And to do it without worrying too much about possible reactions and what others think.

You have to believe you deserve success. You deserve happiness, to be treated well. You deserve to live life on your own terms, not those dictated by others. You deserve to enjoy your work.

So, what does it mean to be fully unleashed?

It is showing up as you, not the 'you' someone else wants you to be. Not who employers told you to be. Not the 'you' lurking in the shadows, fearful of a hypothetical reaction.

You are stepping out, and representing your values, ideas, creativity, thoughts … your best self. The you that is an expert in your field (notice the air quotes have gone). The you that is comfortable with yourself and talks about how far you have come. The you that provides value and support to others, embracing your inner mentor. It is dropping the mask that the evils of employment made you wear.

I approached this in baby steps for quite a while, before I seemed to wake up one day and be all "HELLO! I'M HERE. WITH BUNNIES. AND LOOK AT MY SLOTH." (No, not a euphemism.) I am not entirely sure what the defining moment was that led to this. Maybe it was just that enough time had passed, and enough people had asked me why I even cared what people from my past thought. Why I was still letting previous employers and colleagues have control over me. Why I was still letting their somewhat invisible presence still stop me fully being myself.

It is showing up as you, not the 'you' someone else wants you to be

Good question.

So, I started doing whatever felt right for me, and soon no one could get me to shut up. But it takes time and practice to get there. I asked our relative newbie to self-employment, Kate, if she feels she can be herself in her business yet, and she says, "To a degree. It is early days for my business. I still view it as a business and separate to my personal life but I am much less bothered about crossovers." That is where many will start, and stay, for a while, as they find their feet, though I have noticed Kate blossoming and unleashing her amazing sense of humour more each time I see her, which is just lovely to see.

I may be the minority in gaining momentum as the Prosecco-fuelled, clumsy sod (the two not necessarily always linked) who prances about in a huge fluffy-bunny-eared hat on demand. But I found a balance between being known as an expert in my field and for being helpful, fun to work with and providing a reliable, creative and flexible service to customers. (Check out those values of mine right there.) I know when to be 'serious', and when I can be daft, and there is a balance that can work.

I may be the minority in gaining momentum as the Prosecco-fuelled, clumsy sod who prances about in a huge fluffy-bunny-eared hat on demand

It is so much more fun to conduct business this way. It allows any pretences to fall away, and establishes a rapport quicker with others. It can also aid memorability. The last thing you want as a business owner is to be totally forgettable within seconds of someone meeting you. If I am talked about as 'oh, that genius-something lady with the rabbits, yes she knew her stuff' (actual quote), that's fine by me.

It is all a journey. This is my journey, and yours will likely be starkly different. Your best outcomes appear from taking your time, reflecting, experimenting, adapting, collaborating and doing it your way. From giving yourself permission to change, by committing to the process.

Commit to making a change, and your success will come. I believe that and I hope you do too.

273

Commit to it as if your life and business depend on it. Commit to it like my bunnies commit to parsley. Like I could happily commit to Hugh Jackman.

Joelle's growth is an inspiring demonstration of the journey. "The more I concentrated on the new life and business I was building, the better I felt. Within 12 months of handing in my notice, I was completely recovered; no symptoms, no drugs, no more therapy and, most importantly, I found the real me and that, actually, I quite liked myself."

Commit to making a change. Commit to it like my bunnies commit to parsley

To hear that transformation gives me goosebumps. I relate. Self-employment is a life-changing leap to make.

It is stories like this that give others just starting out on their journey hope. I was fuelled by such stories when I started out, and I hope you feel the collective strength in all the stories that have been shared in the book too. Hurrah.

Good luck. Let's take the new climb, one ladder rung at a time. I hope to see you on the other side.

You're bloody brilliant, you.

(And don't forget it.)

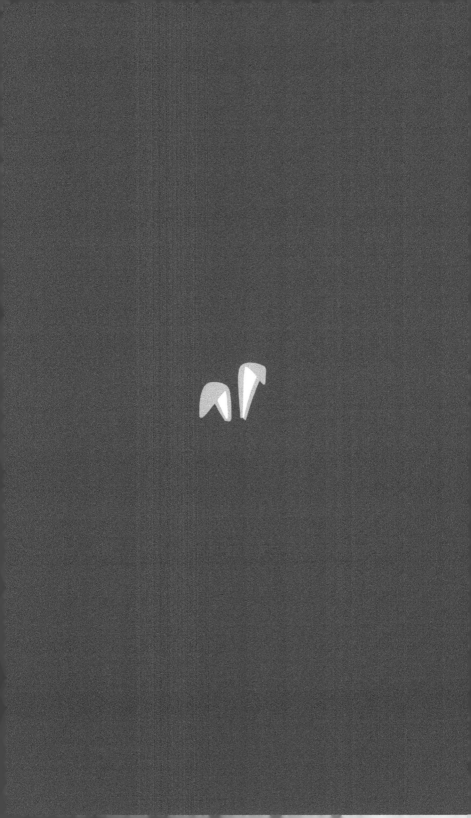

I MARVEL AT HOW WILDLY
DIFFERENT EACH OF [OUR]
STORIES IS. IT'S PROOF
THAT OUR LIVES WERE NEVER
MEANT TO BE COOKIE-
CUTTER, CULTURALLY
CONSTRUCTED CARBON
COPIES OF SOME IDEAL...
THE NORMS WERE CREATED
BY SOMEBODY. EACH OF US
IS SOMEBODY. WE CAN MAKE
YOUR OWN NORMAL. WE CAN
THROW OUT ALL THE RULES
AND WRITE OUR OWN. WE CAN
BUILD OUR LIVES FROM THE
INSIDE OUT. WE CAN STOP
ASKING WHAT THE WORLD

WANTS FROM US AND
INSTEAD ASK OURSELVES
WHAT WE WANT FOR OUR
WORLD. WE CAN STOP
LOOKING AT WHAT'S IN
FRONT OF US LONG ENOUGH
TO DISCOVER WHAT'S
INSIDE US. WE CAN
REMEMBER AND UNLEASH
THE LIFE-CHANGING,
RELATIONSHIP-CHANGING,
WORLD-CHANGING POWER
OF OUR OWN IMAGINATION.
IT MIGHT TAKE A LIFETIME.
LUCKILY, A LIFETIME IS
EXACTLY HOW LONG WE HAVE.

GLENNON DOYLE, UNTAMED[78]

REFERENCES

Part 1: Someone greased the rungs!

1   Breathe HR, "Culture Economy Report", 17 April, 2020; https://www.
    breathehr.com/en-gb/resources/culture-economy-report-2021
2   Drew Rozell, *Write Like This, Not Like That*, 2021, Kindle edition;
    https://www.bookin90days.com
3   SHRM, "Employee Job Satisfaction and engagement: The doors of
    opportunity are open", 24 April, 2017; https://www.shrm.org/hr-
    today/trends-and-forecasting/research-and-surveys/pages/2017-
    job-satisfaction-and-engagement-doors-of-opportunity-are-open.
    aspx
4   OnRec, *Third of UK employees disappointed with their career
    progression*, 15 March, 2016; https://www.onrec.com/news/
    statistics-and-trends/third-of-uk-employees-disappointed-with-
    their-career-progression
5   Meena Alexander, "The Great Reset: Why We All Fell Out Of Love
    With The Career Ladder", *Stylist Magazine*; https://www.stylist.co.uk/
    digital-magazine/issue-551/518555
6   Liz Ryan, "Job Security Is Disappearing - What Does It Mean
    For You?", *Forbes*, 23 May, 2017; https://www.forbes.com/sites/
    lizryan/2017/05/23/job-security-is-disappearing-what-does-it-
    mean-for-you
7   Glennon Doyle, *Untamed: Stop Pleasing, Start Living*, Penguin
    Random House, 2020; page 6
8   Grace Marshall, *Struggle: The surprising truth, beauty and
    opportunity hidden in life's sh*ttier moments*, Kindle edition, Practical
    Inspiration Publishing, 2021; page 85
9   PwC, "Millennials at Work:Reshaping the workplace"; https://www.
    pwc.com/co/es/publicaciones/assets/millennials-at-work.pdf . 2011;
    page 3
10 @yoloakili, "Sometimes I wake up", 18 November, 2019; https://
    twitter.com/YoloAkili/status/1196462901923500035

Part 2: Making the leap. Landing the fall.

11 Grace Marshall, *Struggle: The surprising truth, beauty and opportunity hidden in life's sh*ttier moments*, Kindle edition, Practical Inspiration Publishing, 2021; page 205
12 World Economic Forum. The Future of Jobs Part 1, Chapter 1: The Future of Jobs and Skills. 2016. Available from: https://reports. weforum.org/future-of-jobs-2016/chapter-1-the-future-of-jobs-and-skills/

Part 3: New ascent. New rules.

13 Tom Albrighton, *The Freelance Introvert*, ABC Business Communications Ltd, Norwich, 2020; page 36
14 Grace Marshall, *Struggle: The surprising truth, beauty and opportunity hidden in life's sh*ttier moments*, Kindle edition, Practical Inspiration Publishing, 2021; page 38
15 Denise Duffield-Thomas, *Chillpreneur*, Kindle edition, Hay House UK, 2019; page xiv
16 Glennon Doyle, *Untamed: Stop Pleasing, Start Living*, Penguin Random House, 2020; page 50
17 Grace Marshall, *Struggle: The surprising truth, beauty and opportunity hidden in life's sh*ttier moments*, Kindle edition, Practical Inspiration Publishing, 2021; page 126
18 Elizabeth Gilbert, *Big Magic: Creative Living Beyond Fear*, Bloomsbury, London, 2015; page 150
19 Maria Popova, "Fixed vs. Growth: The Two Basic Mindsets That Shape Our Lives"; https://www.brainpickings.org/2014/01/29/carol-dweck-mindset
20 Elizabeth Gilbert, *Big Magic: Creative Living Beyond Fear*, Bloomsbury, London, 2015; page 125
21 Ed Callow, Write52 Hall of Fame; https://www.write52.com/the-hall-of-fame
22 20th Century Fox, *The Greatest Showman*, "This Is Me", with Keala Settle; https://www.youtube/XLFEvHWD_NE
23 Brené Brown, quoted in Joanna Martin, "When boundaries don't work"; https://oneofmany.co.uk/blog/when-boundaries-dont-work/

24 Grace Marshall, *Struggle: The surprising truth, beauty and opportunity hidden in life's sh*ttier moments*, Kindle edition, Practical Inspiration Publishing, 2021; page 39

25 Brené Brown, quoted in Joanna Martin, "When boundaries don't work"; https://oneofmany.co.uk/blog/when-boundaries-dont-work/

26 Brené Brown, quoted in Joanna Martin, "When boundaries don't work"; https://oneofmany.co.uk/blog/when-boundaries-dont-work/

27 @Katieuniacke; https://www.instagram.com/katieuniacke

28 Denise Duffield-Thomas, *Chillpreneur*, Kindle edition, Hay House UK, 2019; page 19

29 Roar Training, "State of the Workplace Report", 12 May, 2021; https://roar.training/2021-state-of-the-workplace-report

30 @talkingshrimpnyc, "Charge your worth", 23 June, 2021; https://www.instagram.com/p/CQdsR36nSAf

31 IPSE, "Men earn 43% more than women in self-employment"; https://www.business-money.com/announcements/men-earn-43-per-cent-more-than-women-in-self-employment

32 @penthemighty, "Oops I did it again", 3 August, 2021; https://twitter.com/penthemighty/status/1422552755227533326

33 Emma Cownley, "How to price a freelance project (PROPERLY!)", 2021; https://youtu.be/x76RWxXVJFg

34 *Work Notes Pricing Guide*; https://worknotes.co.uk/freelance-pricing-guide

35 @digitalwomen, "Self Note! Repeat after me!", 5 May, 2021; https://www.instagram.com/p/COfd0vZnoqW

36 Glennon Doyle, *Untamed: Stop Pleasing, Start Living*, Penguin Random House, 2020; page 201

37 Steve Morgan, *Anti-Sell: Marketing, Lead Generation & Networking Tips for Freelancers Who Hate Sales*, Kindle edition, Self-published 2019; page 198

38 Insight, "Many UK freelancers feel lonely and isolated following leap to self-employment"; https://workplaceinsight.net/many-uk-freelancers-feel-lonely-and-isolated-following-leap-to-self-employment/

39 Steve King, "Coworking is not about workspace – It's about feeling less lonely", *Harvard Business Review*, 28 December, 2017; https://hbr.org/2017/12/coworking-is-not-about-workspace-its-about-

feeling-less-lonely

40   Freelance Heroes, Freelance Heroes Day reflection, 21 May, 2021;
      https://www.facebook.com/groups/freelanceheroes
41   Kate Toon, *Confessions of a Misfit Entrepreneur: How to succeed in
      business despite yourself*, Self-published, Australia, 2017; page 82
42   Helen Tupper and Sarah Ellis, *The Squiggly Career: Ditch the Ladder,
      Discover Opportunity, Design Your Career*, Kindle edition, Penguin,
      2020; page 50
43   Helen Tupper and Sarah Ellis, *The Squiggly Career: Ditch the Ladder,
      Discover Opportunity, Design Your Career*, Kindle edition, Penguin,
      2020; page 63
44   Reuters, "Employees want climate-positive action from companies.
      Here's how they can deliver"; https://www.reutersevents.com/
      sustainability/employees-want-climate-positive-action-companies-
      heres-how-they-can-deliver
45   Feasts & Fables, "The Encouragement Manifesto"; https://www.
      feastsandfables.co.uk/the-encouragement-manifesto
46   Tim Denning, "How To Understand Your True Value And Never Sell
      Yourself Short Again"; https://medium.com/the-mission/how-to-
      understand-your-true-value-and-never-sell-yourself-short-again-
      66d527197608
47   Sarah Townsend, *Survival Skills for Freelancers*, Kindle edition, Self-
      published, 2020; location 1110
48   Paul Jarvis, *Company of One: Why Staying Small is the Next Big Thing
      for Business*, Penguin Business, 2019; pages 94–95
49   Kate Toon, *Confessions of a Misfit Entrepreneur: How to succeed in
      business despite yourself*, Self-published, Australia, 2017; page 82
50   Brené Brown, "The power of vulnerability"; https://youtu.be/
      iCvmsMzlF7o
51   In a post about imposter syndrome, I once made the mistake of
      saying I call my 'imposter monster' Greta as I imagine it scowling at
      me as Greta Thunberg does in the famous picture where she quite
      rightly scowled at then US President Donald Trump. Apparently, in
      doing this, I was defeating feminism in one fell swoop, pulling all
      women down and being anti-anyone on the spectrum or in any way
      'different'. Apparently, I was calling Greta herself a monster. I was an
      evil witch who should immediately apologise to all women and give

myself a talking to. I actually think she is awesome and anyone who can motivate the next generation to save the planet is a hero. This was all massively taken out of context.

52   Follow Clair Stevenson on LinkedIn here: linkedin.com/in/clair-stevenson-38801a32

53   Follow Jo Watson on LinkedIn here: linkedin.com/in/jo-watson-agoodwriteup

54   Helen Hill, "Being visible, breaking down barriers and building a tribe"; https://www.unlikelygenius.com/2020/06/17/being-visible-breaking-down-barriers-and-building-a-tribe

55   CBS, "Lifetime of learning may help prevent dementia", 24 June, 2014; https://www.cbsnews.com/news/lifetime-of-learning-may-help-prevent-dementia

56   Paul Jarvis, *Company of One: Why Staying Small is the Next Big Thing for Business*, Penguin Business, 2019; page 94

57   Lori Greiner, "'Shark Tank' investor: 'Entrepreneurs are the only people who will work 80 hours a week to avoid working 40 hours a week'", *Business Insider*, 13 July, 2016; https://www.businessinsider.com/lori-greiner-shark-tank-entrepreneurs-2016-7?r=US&IR=T

58   Denise Duffield-Thomas, *Chillpreneur*, Kindle version, Hay House UK, 2019; page xix

59   Tom Albrighton, *The Freelance Introvert*, Norwich: ABC Business Communications Ltd, 2020; pages 71–72

60   Sara Knight, *F**k No! How to stop saying yes when you can't, you shouldn't, or you just don't want to*, Quercus, 2019; pages 3–4

61   No Fucks Given Guides, "Do I really have to?" Flowchart; http://nofucksgivenguides.com/downloads/

62   Honor Clement-Hayes, Freelance Heroes Day 2020, conference proceedings, 6 November, 2020; online

63   Erik Kessels, *Failed It! How to turn mistakes into ideas and other advice for successfully screwing up*, Phaidon Press, 2016; page 87

64   Denise Duffield-Thomas, *Chillpreneur*, Kindle edition, Hay House UK, 2019; page 87

65   Denise Duffield-Thomas, *Chillpreneur*, Kindle edition, Hay House UK, 2019; page xxii

66   John Hegarty, *Hegarty on Creativity: There are No Rules*, Thames & Hudson, 2014; page 104

67 Sarah Townsend, *Survival Skills for Freelancers*, Kindle edition, Self-published, 2020; location 2014

68 Erik Kessels, *Failed It! How to turn mistakes into ideas and other advice for successfully screwing up*, Phaidon Press, 2016; page 4

69 Check Alice out at alicehollis.co.uk

70 Check Dee out at wickedcreative.co.uk

71 Check out Content By The Sea at contentbythesea.co.uk

72 Check out Penny Brazier at the-mighty-pen.co.uk

73 Penny Brazier, "How the pandemic destroyed my creativity and how I rebuilt it brick by brick"; https://penthemighty.medium.com/how-the-pandemic-destroyed-my-creativity-and-how-i-rebuilt-it-brick-by-brick-fe88b3591dbe

74 Penny Brazier, "Space Oddity: a tribute to Bowie's bulge"; https://penthemighty.medium.com/space-oddity-a-tribute-to-bowies-bulge-d468f60524d0

75 Read more about Sophie Cross at thoughtfully.co.uk/sophie-cross

76 Paul Jarvis, *Company of One: Why Staying Small is the Next Big Thing for Business*, Penguin Business, 2019; page 202

THIS IS ME!

77 Glennon Doyle, *Untamed: Stop Pleasing, Start Living*, Penguin Random House, 2020; page 200

78 Glennon Doyle, *Untamed: Stop Pleasing, Start Living*, Penguin Random House, 2020; page 71

RECOMMENDED RESOURCES

All-rounders

Not just a community, you can also find podcasts, networking, Twitter chats, a book club, courses, conferences, masterminds, and so on. Join their Facebook groups, check out the websites and go from there.

* Freelance Heroes – www.freelance-heroes.com
* Being Freelance – www.beingfreelance.com
* The Freelance Lifestyle – www.freelancelifestyle.co.uk

Books

Check out all those in the references list, but particularly my faves:

* *Struggle: The surprising truth, beauty and opportunity hidden in life's sh*ttier moments* by Grace Marshall
* *The Squiggly Career: Ditch the ladder, Discover opportunity, Design your career* by Helen Tupper and Sarah Ellis
* *A Manual For Being Human* by Dr Sophie Mort
* *Survival Skills for Freelancers: Tried and Tested Tips to Help You Ace Self-Employment Without Burnout* by Sarah Townsend
* *Company of One* by Paul Jarvis
* *Untamed* by Glennon Doyle
* *Big Magic* by Elizabeth Gilbert

Mental health and mindset books

There are so many we could be here forever. I shall put a more extensive list on the FOTL website blog, but for now:

* Jenny Lawson – *Furiously Happy* is my favourite, but *Broken* and *Let's Pretend This Never Happened* are also amazing
* *The Anxiety Solution* by Chloe Brotheridge
* *The Miracle of Mindfulness* by Thich Nhat Hanh (or anything by him!)
* *Mindfulness: A Practical Guide to Finding Peace in a Frantic World* by Mark G Williams

- *Self-Compassion* by Kristin Neff
- *Reasons to Stay Alive* by Matt Haig (or, again, any of his stuff)
- *Wintering: How I learned to flourish when life became frozen* by Katherine May (so beautiful!)
- *My Sh*t Therapist & other mental health stories* by Michelle Thomas

Course
- Being Freelance: How to get started being freelance – school.beingfreelance.com/p/how-to-get-started-being-freelance

Podcasts
- The 15 Minute Freelancer by Louise Shanahan
- Happy Place by Fearne Cotton
- The Calmer You by Chloe Brotheridge
- Mind Over Grind by Alice Lyons

Communities and networks
- Mission Led Content with Lisa Barry – www.lisabarryonline.com
- Write Now with Erin Chamberlain – www.facebook.com/writenowwitherinchamberlain
- The Northern Affinity – www.thenorthernaffinity.co.uk
- Videotastic by Becky Holmes – www.becky-holmes.com
- Write52 – www.write52.com

Resources
- Work Notes Freelance Pricing Guide – www.worknotes.co.uk/freelance-pricing-guide
- Kiss My A's by Emma Cownley – www.youtube.com/channel/UCtK8SaYyDKSrcqrWMlhHChg
- Freelancer Magazine – www.freelancermagazine.co.uk
- Tools for Freelancers by Emma Cossey – www.freelancelifestyle.co.uk/resources

ACKNOWLEDGEMENTS

To my Geeg – who is there for the celebrations, tears, highs, lows, laughs, childish antics, and to pick me up when I fall down the stairs ... again (must nearly be double figures now). Often ready with Prosecco, my dinner, a 'nightcap' and the latest bit of wit he has mulled over for hours/days/weeks, just waiting for his moment to launch it to the sound of my groans. I know you hate smushiness, Geeg, but that makes this all the more sweet to say it in print – love you and thank you for everything.

To my family – we are small but we are mighty.

(And we've all fallen off an actual ladder at some point – oh, except you, Myrtle! Stay away from the ladders.) You have cheered me, as I fallen off every rung and gotten back up again. I hope I make you proud. Your support has meant everything and is the catalyst for where I am now.

Especially you, Gandadbun. I know you are looking down and are the proudest daddy.

To Erin Chamberlain, my book mentor (is this what we decided we were calling you?) and editor – if it wasn't for you, I would have been writing totally the wrong book. And thank you for reining me in from the 'research' part of this project (or, more accurately, finding any excuse to read ALL the books in a bid to stave off the fear of actually seeing this through).

To my book designers, Vanessa Mendozzi (cover) and Hannah Beatrice (internal design) – well, what can I say? You nailed it! The response to the design has been incredible. You have both perfectly captured the message of the book.

To my proofreader, Yasmin Yarwood – you haven't even had your mitts on the book yet as I write this, but I have no doubt that you are about to do a cracking job. Apologies for my made-up words. And the length of it.

To my beta readers, Sally and Francesca – what a task you were given, but you pulled it off. Your feedback has been invaluable to me, and is appreciated more than you know.

To my VA, Susanne Wakefield – thank you for putting up with my sporadic organisation and jumbled instructions, and for regularly unfudging my brain. You have been a great support in managing the business and simultaneously getting this book to fruition. You rock.

To all the contributors to this book – a huge thank you to you all for your resounding 'Yes!' to my pleas to get involved. I am still bowled over by your responses, and by the fact that you were all so prompt with your missives (levels of promptness I feel only freelancers achieve). This book would not be the same without your honest and open input, giving some balance to my wonky ways and somewhat meandering story. You guys and gals are amazing.

To the freelance and self-employed communities who put up with my random questions, rants and multitude of bunny pictures – you have been my rock this last two years. Keep doing what you do.

Finally, the book would not be complete without mentioning the bunnies – Tiffin and Strudel. They have been my sanity saver throughout self-employment and make me smile even on the toughest of days. They pick me up and keep me going, and put up with all (some of) my antics and prodding. Sometimes. No doubt their diva levels will soar now.

Lightning Source UK Ltd.
Milton Keynes UK
UKHW022229201021
392547UK00005B/75

9 781919 638508